EDUCATION TODAY: LANGUAGE TEACHING

The Visual Element in Language Teaching

KU-245-656

EDUCATION TODAY

Other titles in this series

An Introduction to the Child Care Service
Social Science and Social Studies in Secondary Schools
Communication in Speech
Student Guidance
Programmed Learning in the Schools
A Basic Science Course for Secondary Schools
Introducing Social Studies
An Approach to Literature
Investment in Children
Living Speech in the Primary School
Development through Drama
Social Learning and its Measurement
An Introduction to the Philosophy of Religion

EDUCATION TODAY: LANGUAGE TEACHING

Teaching English to Immigrants

The Visual Element in Language Teaching

S. PIT CORDER
Head of the Department of Applied Linguistics
University of Edinburgh

LONGMANS

EDINBURGH UNIVERSITY LIBRARY
WITHDRAWN

LONGMANS, GREEN AND CO LTD
48 Grosvenor Street, London W1.
*Associated companies, branches and representatives
throughout the world*

© S. Pit Corder 1966
First published 1966

*Printed in Great Britain by
The Camelot Press Ltd.,
London and Southampton*

Contents

Introduction   ix

1 Language in Learning   1

2 Language Teaching and Meaning   6
  1 The Learning of Language
  2 Meaning
  3 The Teaching of Meaning

3 The Visual Element in Language Teaching   32
  1 Visual Materials
  2 Visual Materials and the Teacher
  3 Relevant Features in Visual Materials
  4 Seeing, Recognising and Understanding Visual Material

4 The Use of Visual Materials   59
  1 Situational Teaching
  2 Sound Film
  3 Audio-visual Courses
  4 Television

  Conclusion   93

Acknowledgements

We are grateful to the following for permission to reproduce copyright material:

The British Council for extracts from the dialogue of *What's the Time?* (a film by Basic Films Ltd—Producer, John Krish), and for extracts from the accompanying *Notes for the Teacher*; Macmillan & Co. Ltd for the extracts from *Composition Exercises in Elementary English* by A. S. Hornby, and the Ministry of Education (Inspectorate Division), Ibadan, for extracts from the *Experimental Language Teaching Programme for Schools*, broadcast in Ibadan on 10th November, 1960—Producer George Arms.

Introduction

Nihil in intellectu quod non fuit prius in sensu (Aristotle)

This quotation from Aristotle, freely translated, means: there is
nothing in knowledge which has not first passed through the
senses. It is printed in this, its Latin, form on the title page of one
of the numerous English editions of Comenius'[1] famous language
teaching text book, the *Orbis Sensualium Pictus*, or *The Visible
World in Pictures*. He goes on to quote it approvingly in his
preface. Aristotle realised that our only contact with the world
outside ourselves was through our senses and that therefore they
were the gateway to all knowledge, but it was Comenius who first
seems to have understood what this meant for language teaching,
and, in particular, for *the teaching of meaning*.

By means of our senses we learn about our environment;
through them we learn to adapt ourselves to it; through them we
communicate by means of language with our fellow men. But we
also use language to learn about our environment. For example,
until recently, nearly all formal teaching was carried out through
the medium of language. But in recent years educators have come
to lay more emphasis on learning through the senses, and
particularly through the sense of sight, since it appears that the
great majority of us learn more readily through that sense than
through any of the others. The methods of teaching which make
use of the learner's sense of sight as well as language are often
known as *visual methods* and many of the materials the teacher
uses in these methods are called *visual aids*.

It is now almost taken for granted that visual methods of
teaching get better results than methods which depend exclusively
upon language. It is also very often taken for granted that visual
methods are equally effective in the teaching of all subjects, for
example, that, because we can show that these methods are

---

[1] Comenius is the Latinised form of the name Komensky; Johann Amos
Komensky was a celebrated Moravian educational reformer of the seventeenth
century. He wrote several revolutionary books on language teaching, of which
the *Orbis Sensualium Pictus* (1658) was the last.

particularly effective in teaching science, they will also be just as effective in the teaching of languages. Now, knowledge of what is sometimes called a 'content' subject, such as science, is generally considered to be a body of facts and concepts, while the knowledge of a language is better thought of as a set of skills. Consequently, the assumption that visual methods are equally effective in teaching language and 'content' subjects needs questioning, and, if possible, theoretical justification; it requires, in other words, a *rationale*. This is what this book attempts to offer.

The argument will be that visual methods are indeed more efficient than those relying wholly upon language, but that the reason why this is so in language teaching is quite different from the reason that it is so in teaching a 'content' subject such as geography or zoology.

The explanation is to be found in the relationship between language and the world outside language. This is the central problem of *meaning*, with which philosophers and psychologists have always been concerned. They have now been joined by the linguists.

Living languages were taught until fairly recently largely through language, while dead languages, like Latin, Greek and Sanskrit, were taught entirely through language; these methods have come to be known as Grammar-Translation methods. In these, the senses played little or no part in learning (except, of course, for hearing and seeing words). In this respect, one must admit, the teaching of languages was more or less in line with the teaching of 'content' subjects.

Nowadays, however, in teaching a 'content' subject, knowledge is most often imparted through a combination of sensory experience and language; in other words, by *audio-visual* means. These could be illustrated in this way:

In teaching language the same three elements are involved, but the relationships are different:

DIRECT SENSORY EXPERIENCE ⇌ KNOWLEDGE OF THE WORLD
↓
LANGUAGE

In the two sorts of learning the 'unknown' factor is different; in the first it is *knowledge* which is absent and has to be attained; in the second it is *language*. In the first, the relationship between sensory experience and language is taken for granted, that is, the learner is assumed to know his language. It is assumed that there is no problem of meaning.[1] In the second, the relationship between sensory experience and knowledge is assumed, and it is the relationship between these two and language that has to be learned. But this is the relationship which we have just called the central problem of meaning, so it comes about that, whenever we teach language, *meaning* is what we are concerned with.

The linguist has a dictum: All study of language is the study of meaning, or as the British linguist Dr. Halliday puts it:[2]

For the linguist, all study and description of language, whether formal or contextual, is concerned with meaning, since language is meaningful behaviour. (My translation)

We do not teach language for its own sweet sake, as if it were an aesthetically satisfying logical system, like mathematics. We teach language so that our pupils can communicate and be communicated with, so that they may convey meaning and understand meaning, so that they may enter into satisfactory mutual relations with native speakers or writers of the language. The teacher's dictum must be: All teaching of language is the teaching of meaning.

[1] I am excluding the situation where a *second* language is also the medium of instruction in 'content' subjects. This happens in the large number of 'English Medium Schools' all over the world. In the examples we have given, only one of the elements is 'unknown' but where we are teaching knowledge and simultaneously teaching language there are two unknown 'elements'. In this case the techniques of teaching are more difficult because the only thing we can take for granted is the learner's sensory experience.

[2] M. A. K. Halliday: 'Linguistique Générale et Linguistique Appliquée' in *Etudes de Linguistique Appliquée*, I. Didier, Paris 1962.

I

Language in Learning

Whatever we may believe the educational process to be, we must all agree that it involves becoming acquainted with our physical and social environment. We can get this knowledge of the world outside ourselves either *directly* through our senses or *indirectly* through communication with other people, that is through language, as a rule. These two ways of learning have been called learning through *experience* and learning through *information*,[1] or as in the following quotation from J. B. Carroll,[2] the Harvard educational psychologist, *inductive* and *deductive* learning:

> One procedure can be called inductive; it consists of presenting an individual with an appropriate series of positive and negative instances, labeled as such, and allowing him to infer the nature of the concept. . . .
> Another procedure for concept teaching may be called deductive and it tends to be the favored procedure in school learning. It is the technique of presenting concepts by verbal definition or description.

Experience itself is no more than a series of sensory impressions; experience does not become knowledge until these impressions are organised in some way. Organised sensory impressions are sometimes called concepts. For example impressions of roundness, smoothness, shininess and rosiness are organised into our idea of an apple, so that when we have these or similar sensations in the future we recognise an apple. Information on the other hand is knowledge not acquired through one's own senses but through those of another person. We could then also learn the idea of an apple, if we had never seen one, by being informed by someone

[1] Richard Palmer: 'Experience, Information and the Mass Media', *The Year Book of Education, 1960*, Evans, 1960.
[2] John B. Carroll: *Words, Meanings and Concepts, Harvard Educational Review*, Special Issue: Language and Learning, 34, II (1964).

who had that an apple was a round, smooth, shiny, rosy fruit.

Now in the absence of learning by information, a learner will, of course, whether he likes it or not, start to organise his own experiences, that is, to form his own concepts. This is not necessarily a deliberate and conscious process. Concept-formation of this sort leads to knowledge which, since it has been obtained by the learner's unaided effort, is better learned and more firmly retained.

This fact is worth remembering, because when later the learning of meaning is discussed, we shall see that if the learner works out the meaning of a bit of foreign language for himself, he learns it much better than when he is 'given' the meaning by his teacher, i.e. by translation.

However, although this process of concept-formation is the very foundation of knowledge, it is often liable to be a slow one, and more seriously, an uncertain one, since the learner, through inaccurate observation and incomplete experience, can easily form inadequate concepts. For example, unless a child has someone who can tell him that what he has decided, on the basis of his experience, to call an apple, is *really* an example of that fruit, he may get the idea that oranges are also a sort of apple. Anyone who has had to do with young children will be familiar with this phenomenon. If a learner forms a wrong concept of this sort, he will sooner or later have to abandon or alter it, and this will be all the more difficult for him to do, because, as we have said, those concepts formed by the learner for himself are the most firmly retained.

One of the teacher's main duties is to help and guide the learner in forming the correct concepts, and in doing so economically and quickly. The teacher may do this in two ways: by putting the learner in the way of receiving sensory experience in a manner and sequence which will enable him to form correct concepts for himself most quickly, or by the judicious giving of information. These are the two ways referred to by Carroll in the quotation given above.

Since the development of modern communications by sea, land and air, and since the invention of radio, film and television, the learner's potential environment has been extended to include virtually the whole world. All of us are now subject in our daily lives to the influence of what happens on the other side of the globe. Yet it is clearly impossible for us to have direct, un-mediated experience of anything but a minute part of this environment. An equally important part of our environment is the culture and history of our own community. Here again the amount we can learn by unmediated sensory experience is limited and we have to rely upon learning through information.

While modern communications have extended the environ-ment of each one of us, they have also in the process of doing so offered the learner a way of learning about this environment through sensory experience; but with this difference, that what he may experience directly is selected for him and comes to him through only two of his senses, sight and hearing. The mass media of communication are *audio-visual*. Furthermore this mediated experience nearly always comes accompanied by information.

So far we have spoken of information and experience as if they were in contrast to each other. They are, in fact, usually comple-mentary. It is rare that direct experience in the classroom is not accompanied, or at least immediately followed, by information covering the same field and organising the sensory impressions just received.

Furthermore, although information is normally mediated by language, it need not always be so. Much ready-conceptualised information is brought to the learner by other means: for example, in diagrams, maps, charts, graphs or models. It can often happen that these visual means of conveying information are more effective than language. A map is an example of this. No one can learn the shape of a country from direct experience, and to describe the shape in words would be very difficult.

Direct experience and information usually come together in formal learning and through the mass media of communication. In this way the learner attains new concepts or knowledge. Further understanding of his environment is gained by a repetition of the same process, when fresh experience and information combine with existing knowledge to form new and more generalised concepts. So the process of learning goes on through life. The important thing is that there must always be a

3

component of direct sensory experience in this learning—a sort of verification procedure—or else learning develops into what philosophers call a logical system (mathematics is one of these) and the learner loses touch with reality.

We can now see more clearly where language enters into the learning process; it is the means whereby ready-made concepts are communicated to the learner. Its object is to help the learner to organise the experience he has had and the concepts he has formed into new abstractions. It also gives him the linguistic means to discuss with others, and to record, the concepts he has attained.

Here lies a danger. It is all too easy for information to be supplied to the learner which he cannot relate to his own experience or to the knowledge he has so far acquired. He may then acquire the linguistic forms (usually lexical) without the concepts with which they should be associated, that is, which give them meaning. This is often called *verbalism* and is characterised by the learner's using language which he does not himself fully understand; in other words, it results in parrot-learning.

Comenius said about verbalism, that 'no one should be allowed to talk about anything he does not understand'. As we shall see later, certain procedures in second language teaching, if used unwisely, tend to produce similar results.

In the same passage Comenius goes on to say that 'no one should be allowed to understand anything without at the same time being able to express his knowledge in words'. By this he meant that the process of learning about the world must always be accompanied by the ability to talk about what we have learnt. This notion is also important because it stresses the way in which concept formation and language are inextricably mixed. We never tire of telling ourselves that what distinguishes us from even the highest of the animals is our ability to form abstract concepts. This is often expressed as 'man's unique possession of language'. We might equally well say that our power to form abstract concepts is the result of our possession of language. In fact, the two develop together in the growth and maturation of the individual. We shall see that this is so in the next chapter.

We have also seen that information can come to us visual**y** through diagrams. It is thus no accident that all writing systems have apparently developed from drawings.

When someone learns a language, he is not, properly speaking, gaining a knowledge of his environment. Language is not knowledge, but a set of skills. The teaching of it, therefore, must be different from the teaching of a 'content' subject like science, and the role of direct sensory experience in the learning of a language will also therefore be different.

2

Language Teaching and Meaning

Section I The Learning of Language

At the end of the last chapter language was called part of human behaviour and the learning of it was said to be the learning of a set of skills. Of course, it is possible to study language or languages in the way we study history or geography or a science—as a 'content' subject, a set of concepts of varying degrees of abstraction. This is the way a linguist studies a language, so that he can analyse and describe it. This, too, requires skill, but it is the sort of skill a scientist needs rather than the language learner; there is many an academic linguist who is capable of giving an excellent description of a language in which he may be only a mediocre performer.

The skills of performance and those of description are different, and the most intensive descriptive study of a language does not necessarily lead to an ability to communicate in or understand that language. It may, in certain circumstances, particularly with highly educated adult learners, help to do so, but it is not a necessary or intrinsic part of learning a language. This is shown by the fact that all people without exception learn to communicate by means of their mother-tongue with no, or, at the best, very little teaching *about* their own language.

Most aspects of everyday behaviour, including language, are learnt to a high degree of skill without any formal teaching. We have all learned, for example, to eat, walk and sleep without having been instructed in the physiological, psychological or anatomical aspects of those activities. We were taught them as skills, as behaviour, but not as a body of knowledge.

Languages, then, can be learnt without the learner being given a linguistic description of the language, and learning a language is learning a set of skills. This much is now becoming generally accepted, though not yet always acted upon.

There was once a 'method' of teaching languages which got the

name 'The Natural Method'. The theory underlying it was that
if we could learn a second language in the way we learned our
mother-tongue, all our problems would be at an end. This
notion has been largely abandoned, not because it was untrue, but
because the method was impossible. Even if we could succeed in
recreating, in the case of a second language, the emotional
environment and developmental conditions in which an infant
learns its first language, we should be dealing with merely
another first language, or second mother-tongue, not a foreign or
second language. Millions of people in the world do learn a
second mother-tongue in this way; bi-linguals are common in
many societies.

It is precisely because we cannot reproduce the situation of
mother-tongue learning in all or even most of its aspects when
teaching second languages to older children or adults that we
have a second language problem at all.

But when this has been said, it must not thereafter be assumed
that we cannot learn anything useful for second language teaching
from a study of the way a child learns its mother-tongue. Indeed
it is from the increased interest on the part of linguists and
psychologists in this aspect of child development that a clearer
understanding of what the linguistic skills are has developed.

Another source of information about language skills has been
the neurologist who studies those disorders called aphasias, in
which language performance can be impaired in a large number
of different ways.

From these studies it has become possible to build up a model
of the language skills which helps to explain the experiences of
the language teacher in the classroom and the ways he has come
empirically to find the most effective in teaching a second
language.

Anyone who has had to do with the learning or teaching of a
language knows that the ability to express himself in the language
and the ability to understand the language, while connected, are
nevertheless partly distinct abilities. He finds that some people
appear to have greater skill in expression than in understanding,
whilst others appear to understand well and yet remain virtually
incapable of expressing themselves. This common experience

B   7

suggests that language skills can be broadly classified into productive and receptive. This impression is indeed fully borne out
by the neurologist, who finds that these skills are indeed very
largely separate and in certain speech disorders the productive
skill may be totally impaired without the receptive skill being
affected.

This main division of the skills is, of course, a familiar one. But
the further traditional division into writing, speaking, reading and
hearing skills, whilst having some value, does not tell us nearly
enough to help us in our teaching. Indeed, as long as forty years
ago the famous neurologist Henry Head said of 'speech', 'reading',
'writing' and 'memory for words' that they are purely verbal
descriptions of certain human actions and that there is no reason
to suppose that these terms correspond to any distinct and
separate groups of psychological functions.

A more satisfactory division of the language skills for teaching
purposes will be threefold. The first group of skills are what can
be called the *motor-perceptive skills*. The motor skills are those
concerned with the articulation of speech sounds and the manual
work of forming letters, whilst the perceptive skills are those concerned with the recognition of sounds (auditory) and marks on
paper (visual). These skills have to be taught, of course, and much
time is necessarily spent upon them, particularly in the earlier
stages of language learning. The ability to make and distinguish
between the different marks on paper is a skill which is often
learnt first in the mother-tongue, and is transferred direct to the
second language. (If both use the same alphabet or syllabary.)
But this is never the case at the phonetic level. We always have to
teach pronunciation. Notice that here we are concerned with the
ability to distinguish letters and speech sounds, and form them;
we are not concerned with matters of spelling or, say, correct
syllable formation or correct accentuation.

It is quite possible to learn, and presumably to teach, these
motor-perceptive skills in the absence of any of the other linguistic
skills. We not infrequently meet people—often on the music-hall
stage—who have developed these powers of mimicry to a high
degree of efficiency, and who can 'talk' in a manner which
immediately sounds, say, French, without using any French

8

words or French grammar; what they say, of course, has no meaning in the ordinary sense.

The second group of skills are the *organisational skills*. These are concerned with the organising of the units of the language, whether vocabulary units, grammatical units or units of sound such as the syllable or the foot, into acceptable patterns, and, on the other hand, with the ability to discern and analyse such patterns when read or heard. The productive and receptive aspects of these skills can be called generative and analytic respectively.

It is obvious that the learning of the organisational skills must occupy a large part of our time in the classroom; but it is not so obvious that these skills could be learnt without the student learning to communicate effectively or understand what was being said to him in the language. For example, we can teach the student that in English there is a fairly simple system in the way that three consonants may be grouped at the beginning of a syllable

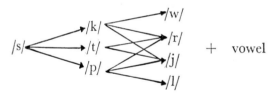

Thus we could construct or generate, for example, /skru:/, /stru:/ and /spru:/, all of which exist as words in English. We can also generate /spri:/ and /skri:/, and */stri:/,[1] which does not occur in English. We can also generate /sprai/, */skrai/ and */strai/, the last two of which do not occur in English. Teaching the organisational skill of phonology alone will not prevent the learner from generating */stri:/ and also */skrai/ and */strai/, all of which follow the 'rules' of English phonology and are thus acceptable patterns.

To take another example, from grammar this time. The suffixes *-ful* and *-less* may be added to a long list of abstract nouns to form

[1] When a linguist wants to talk for any reason about a form which does not exist in a language he marks it with a star.

adjectives; thus from the words *help, use, purpose* and *meaning* we may form *helpful* and *helpless*, *useful* and *useless*, *purposeful* and *purposeless*, and *meaningful* and *meaningless*. No grammatical rules have yet been formulated to prevent the learner forming both *beautiful* and *beautiless, *pointful and *pointless*, *dutiful* and *dutiless, where only one of each pair exists as a word in English.

Teaching the organisational skill alone, then, does not automatically give our learner the ability to communicate, and any attempt to do so would certainly entail a great expense of effort and time, and there would seem to be no possible reason for doing so. The learner would have no motive for learning because, as we have seen, the object of language is the transmission of meaning. Only the academic linguist might have a reason for learning the patterns of a language without also learning their meaning, or, in other words, when to use them.

Nevertheless, it is important to realise that in a limited way this does sometimes happen in learning even the mother-tongue; children often pick up the forms of their mother-tongue without knowing their meaning and generate forms which do not exist; and at school it is not uncommon for teachers to assume that the child has learnt something just because he seems able to use the right words. This is what we have already called verbalism. It also occurs fairly frequently in teaching second languages when the emphasis has been laid too heavily on acquiring good linguistic habits to the neglect of other important aspects of language teaching.

It may at first sight seem absurd that it is possible for someone to appear to talk 'correctly' and even sometimes 'sensibly' without fully knowing what he is saying, but such indeed is the case, for there is a higher level skill which must be developed before a completely meaningful use of language is achieved.

This is the *semantic skill*, and it has to do with the expression of what is usually thought of as meaning. Acceptable words strung together in the acceptable patterns of the language do not by that fact alone have meaning. They have still to be used in the right circumstances to have meaning of an effective sort, and by this I mean to communicate or produce the desired result in the hearer.

Although the existence of such a skill has been largely ignored by the language teacher, its existence as a separate psychological function was recognised by Head, the neurologist already mentioned, when he spoke of a semantic mode of behaviour which, when disturbed, resulted in the want of recognition of the full significance of the words and phrases used by a speaker, apart from their 'direct verbal meaning', by which he presumably meant what some modern linguists call their formal meaning.

This short account of the linguistic skills yields us a picture like this:

LEARNER

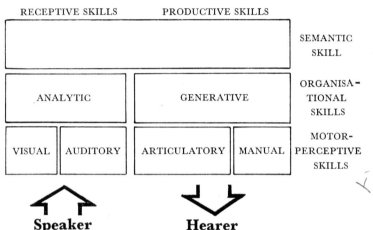

RECEPTIVE SKILLS   PRODUCTIVE SKILLS

		SEMANTIC SKILL
ANALYTIC	GENERATIVE	ORGANISA-TIONAL SKILLS
VISUAL	AUDITORY	ARTICULATORY	MANUAL	MOTOR-PERCEPTIVE SKILLS

Speaker   **Hearer**

Let us now relate this account of the linguistic skills to our activities in the classroom. The emphasis in recent language teaching practice has been on two aspects of language learning. The first of these is a 'good pronunciation'. By this is usually meant a pronunciation as nearly phonetically identical with that of the native speaker as we can achieve. Whether this is a necessary thing or not does not concern us here, but we may note that we do not usually insist that in writing our students should aim at an 'English' or 'French' hand.

The second aspect emphasised nowadays is the learning of 'good linguistic habits'. These are taken to be the ability to produce correct grammatical structures 'unconsciously'.

Let us try to relate 'good pronunciation' and 'good linguistic habits' to the linguistic skills which have been outlined. We shall recognise that 'learning a good pronunciation' is the acquisition of the motor-perceptive skills of speech. As we have remarked already these phonetic skills can be taught in isolation and a course in the practical phonetics of a language would have precisely this as its aim. It is possible to have a good pronunciation without any corresponding ability to speak or understand a language.

The insistence on teaching 'good linguistic habits' is a little more difficult to relate to the skills. In the first place it certainly includes the development of the organisational skills as far as grammar is concerned: that is, the ability to form and distinguish acceptable grammatical patterns. It probably also includes similar organisational skills in the patterning of the sound element: that is, the ability to form and recognise acceptable syllables as we saw just now and also intonation and stress patterns, though some of this is often included under the general heading of a 'good pronunciation'. What 'good linguistic habits' less often include is the systematic teaching of the organisation of lexical patterns. The learning of vocabulary is widely regarded as a separate task which has somehow more to do with meaning than has grammar; this is because it is not yet generally realised that the vocabulary element of a language can be shown to have a structure in the same sense that grammar has.

In grammar, for example, we are able to assign words to a grammatical class by showing that they function in a similar way; thus we may recognise nouns by the fact that they can follow the definite article *the*, e.g. the *money*, the *man*, and the *time*. *Money*, *man* and *time* are all members of the same grammatical class. A lexical class, or set, is identified by a similar procedure. For example, *he cut himself with a knife/razor/axe*, but not *he cut himself with money/a man/* or *the time*. *Knife, razor,* and *axe* belong in the same lexical set because they function lexically in the same way, whilst *money, man* and *time* are not members of the same lexical set because they do not function lexically in the same way.

The whole-hearted pursuit of the organisational skills embodied in the notion of 'learning good linguistic habits' can easily lead to a control of grammatical structure unaccompanied by a corresponding achievement in the semantic skill. We tend to teach our pupils *what* to do, but often neglect to teach them *when* to do it; in other words, we neglect the teaching of meaning.

What is at present done to teach the semantic skill? Vocabulary is popularly regarded as the only meaningful element of a language. Thus the teaching of a vocabulary is normally thought of as the teaching of meaning, and the only teaching of meaning that needs to be done. But as we have just seen, the lexical element of a language has a formal structure in the same way that grammar has, and, furthermore, grammar itself has, in its turn, meaning in the same way as vocabulary has. Thus to regard the teaching of vocabulary as the whole teaching of meaning in language is to disregard an important part of the organisational skills on the one hand, and of the semantic skill on the other. It leads, in short, to only a partial development of both organisational and semantic skills.

There is, then, much more to the development of the semantic skill than the at present rather haphazard and often inefficient teaching of the 'meaning' of words. We need, besides, the teaching of meaning of grammatical items. In fact we need the whole area of meaning to be taught methodically—the conscious, deliberate and systematic development of the semantic skill and nothing less.

The next two sections are concerned with this matter, for it is in this part of language teaching that the visual sense plays a dominant though not exclusive role; it is in this part that teaching language by description is least effective, in which teaching through *information* is less powerful than teaching through *experience.*

Section 11 Meaning

Nothing 'possesses' speed. We cannot speak about the speed of anything in isolation—whether it is a car, an aeroplane, or even the earth. Any one of these has speed only in relation to some other object. If we walk along the corridor of a train, our speed in relation to the train might be two miles an hour, but the train could be standing in the station or going along the track at seventy miles an hour. This makes no difference to our speed in relation to the train; on the other hand, our speed in relation to the earth would be different in each case, and might even depend on the direction in which we were walking.

Nothing in language 'possesses' meaning. We cannot talk about the meaning of anything in isolation—whether it is a word, a phrase, or even a whole sentence. Any one of these has meaning only in relation to some other items of language or features of situational context, and may have several different meanings depending upon the items or features we are relating them to.

The reader will have noticed that these last sentences were an echo of those which started this section. Only a few words were changed: *meaning* for *speed*, *word* for *car* and *item of language* for *object*, etc.

Meaning is, like speed, a relationship. That is why we must beware of talking about the meaning of any word in isolation, as if the word inherently had meaning in the way that objects may have shape or texture, or alternatively, as a container may hold a quantity of material. We must also beware of talking about words, changing their meaning, or widening and narrowing their meaning. All they may do is change the number and nature of the relationships they normally enter into. Furthermore, and most important, words are by no means the only things in a language which are concerned in meaning.

For example, this series of sounds /tendə/, cannot strictly even be called a word until it occurs in a piece of connected speech. Even supposing we assume it to be a word, we still could not assign it to a grammatical class, even less say what its meaning was until it was placed in a linguistic setting, thus:

a I shall *tender* my resignation
b His foot was rather sore and *tender*
c The cargo was loaded into a *tender*

We can see now that *tender* (*a*) is a verb and occurs most often with words like *thanks, apology, condolence,* and can be replaced by such a word as *offer*. *Tender* (*b*) on the other hand is an adjective and occurs more often with words like *finger, hand* or other parts of the body, or with *conscience, heart, feeling*. These evidently form quite a different set from the previous ones. Finally, *tender (c)* occurs with words like *locomotive, engine, load, cargo* and is a noun, again clearly distinguishable from the other two *tenders*.

This notion that meaning is not something which is a possession or inherent quality of words or grammatical items is, of course, a commonplace in modern linguistic theory. For the linguist a word is just a series of noises—organised, admittedly, according to certain rules. It is only when it is found in a setting of some sort that it begins to acquire meaning. This statement by the French linguist Martinet[1] is the sort of remark we may meet in any modern book on language:

A linguistic element has, strictly speaking, meaning only within a context and a given situation.

The usefulness of this quotation for our immediate purposes is that it makes a distinction between *context* and *situation*. We do not need to assume that these two terms are used in quite the same way by all linguists,[2] but the notion that there are two different sorts of setting in which linguistic elements may be found and studied is important, because it suggests that there are two different sets of relationships into which these elements may enter and hence 'acquire meaning'; i.e. become meaningful.

The first sort of setting, called by Martinet *context*, is that made up of the other linguistic items amongst which the element occurs. For example, any vocabulary word is surrounded in a sentence by other words, similarly a letter is surrounded by other letters, or a grammatical form is accompanied by other grammatical forms. This type of context is a linguistic one, or a *formal* one, and is therefore often called the *formal context* of the element we are

[1] A. Martinet: *Elements of General Linguistics*, Faber, 1964.

[2] The two sorts of setting mentioned here are given different names by different linguists. *Context* is often used for both *linguistic* and *non-linguistic* context. We also find these called *formal* and *situational* context respectively, while the latter is sometimes called the *context of situation*. In this book, we are mainly concerned with matters concerning the *situational context*, or, as it may also be called, the *contextual situation*. Both terms are used in this book and elsewhere with the same meaning. The term *contextualise* will mean the demonstration, or placing of bits of language in a situational context.

considering. The relationship of co-occurrence we have just mentioned is an example of a *formal relation* and out of such a relation arises *formal meaning*.

This sort of meaning is, of course, very important, particularly to the linguist. When we learn to form acceptable grammatical or lexical patterns we are at the same time creating a network of *formal* relationships and expressing the *formal* meanings which arise out of them. But we are not directly concerned with them in this book, because they belong in the field of the organisational skills, not the semantic skill.

The sort of meaning we are concerned with here in a book on the visual element in language teaching is the one which has to do with Martinet's *situation*. In this case, the setting in which our linguistic element occurs is not a linguistic one, the other bits of language it is surrounded by, but a non-linguistic one, the people, events and things present when the bit of language is uttered.

The meaning-giving relationships in this case are those between language and the relevant elements in the situation in which it occurs as an element itself, and not between the linguistic form and other forms. This sort of meaning is called *situational meaning*.

The great American linguist, Leonard Bloomfield, went so far as to say that the meaning of a piece of language is 'the situation in which the speaker utters it and the response which it calls forth in the hearer'.[1] This might be regarded as an extreme view by some, but it does help to emphasise the point that we must be careful to avoid thinking of the situational context of language as a sort of moving theatrical back-drop against which the piece of language we are concerned with occurs. Let me here quote from one more great linguist, J. R. Firth:

> The context of situation . . . is not merely a setting or 'back-drop' for the words. The text is regarded as an integral part of the context and is observed in relation to other parts regarded as relevant in the statement of the context.[2]

[1] Leonard Bloomfield: *Language*, Allen & Unwin, 1935.
[2] J. R. Firth: 'A Synopsis of Linguistic Theory, 1930-55', *Studies in Linguistic Analysis*, Blackwell, 1962.

If we were sociologists or psychologists attempting to explain the workings of a situation of human interaction, the verbal element, instead of being, as it is with the linguist, in the centre of attention, would be merely another feature of the situation which was relevant for the explanation of the actions or presence of the participants. The relationships, however, which these other observers would have to take into account would be exactly the same as those the linguist observed in making his statements about the meaning of the language.

After all, language does not simply happen 'in a vacuum'. It is the very complicated response of a speaker or writer to his environment. Viewed in this way, verbal behaviour is no different in kind from any other behaviour. We often see people doing something which we don't understand and which we cannot immediately account for from what we can see. If we continue to watch them, their actions will usually come to make sense to us eventually; sometimes this happens only after they have explained to us in words what they are doing and why. This is often because the cause of the activity and its effect lie outside our knowledge and experience.

Now, the same is true of language behaviour. It is not an uncommon experience for us to overhear a bit of language which we simply do not understand, although it is our mother-tongue and we are familiar with the individual words, the grammatical structures and the intonation and stress patterns. In other words the language is familiar but meaningless.

Why is this possible? If we can understand the reason for this common experience, we shall have gone some way to understanding the notion of situational meaning. Our failure could be explained in two ways: firstly, that the speaker is mentally sick or deficient, and that consequently his verbal behaviour, whilst meaningful to himself, is not so to a listener, because it seems to bear no relation to the situation in which it occurs. This lack of contact between the speaker and reality is a symptom, in fact, of his sickness; it used to be called alienation, a term which emphasised this lack of contact. In the ordinary way, we would dismiss this explanation.

The second explanation is that, although the speaker is a

17

rational human being and his verbal behaviour is indeed related to the situation, we, the observer, are unable to discern the relationship through lack of experience, awareness or knowledge of what he is doing, or who he is or who he is talking to. In other words, a bit of language is meaningful in the degree to which it is related to its situation on the one hand, and is discerned to be so related by a hearer on the other. The casual eavesdropper does not immediately understand what he hears, not because the language is unrelated to the situation, but because he has not perceived the relationship. The longer he listens, however, the more he is able to recognise such a relationship and the more meaningful the language becomes for him. Anyone can demonstrate this to himself by switching on the television set. The sound usually comes up before the picture, and it is quite normal to find that one cannot understand what the talk means until the picture appears and one knows who is speaking to whom, and what they are doing and in what sort of physical surroundings.

Let us go back for a moment to the notion of speed as a relationship between objects. As we walked down the train we had a speed in relation to the carriage, irrespective of the speed the train may have had in relation to the rails. In a similar way, language between speaker and hearer has meaning irrespective of whether an eavesdropper understands it or not. Why? Because the eavesdropper is not in any normal relation to the speaker and hearer. He is not part of the situation in which the language takes place. He will, of course, understand what we called the *formal meaning*; he may even express this fact in such words as: 'It was just so many words to me'. But he will not have understood the *situational meaning*.

When people use language in ordinary, everyday life, it is what they say as a *whole* that is meaningful. This may be just a single word in answer to a question, for example, or it may be a string of sentences lasting an hour, as in a public lecture. We can see that this is so by the strenuous objections that people very often raise to having odd sentences of theirs quoted from a longer context. They rightly point out that the meaning of such a quotation is either unclear or incomplete. These single words or long strings of sentences are what the linguist calls utterances.

Unless some accident or interruption occurs, all our utterances are complete, and from a technical point of view, the shortest utterance must be regarded as a sentence even if it only consists of a single word; indeed, the word has been described as the minimal free utterance—the smallest unit of language which occurs alone in a natural situation. This is why we try to teach language in units of never less than a sentence, and it means that we must accept the fact that our sentences may sometimes consist of only one word. Nevertheless, sentences are usually made up formally of more than one word; they have grammatical structure and carry certain features of pronunciation like intonation and stress. It is natural therefore to wish to break down the meaning of whole sentences into their constituent parts: the meanings of the words used in the sentence, the meaning of the grammar and the meaning of the intonation and the stress. The moment we do this, however, we move back into the field of *formal meaning*. The meaning of a word in a sentence, the meaning of a grammatical structure or an intonation pattern is a matter of formal meaning and only indirectly of situational meaning. Therein lies the difficulty. A big change in a linguistic form is not necessarily associated with a big change in situational meaning and the same linguistic form may have quite different situational meanings on different occasions. When someone says '*That was a sensible thing to do*' it depends largely on the contextual situation whether he meant it was or was not sensible. He might have been speaking ironically. Similarly, in most circumstances at least, the two sentences: *she got John a book from the library* and *she got a book for John from the library*, would be considered to have a similar meaning, and yet grammatically they represent different structures.

A native speaker of a language is always able to give a reasonably good account of both the formal use of a word and the sort of situation in which it is conventionally used, i.e. the dictionary definition.[1] He can do this because he possesses an enormous stock

[1] Actually, when asked to tell someone the meaning of a word he will, often enough, resort to giving a sentence with it in, that is, to giving its formal meaning. In many cases this is much the easiest thing to do, and in some cases the *only* thing to do.

of memories of the different situations in which he has experienced the word. He has, by this means, gradually built up an abstract picture, a meaning scheme, of the type of situation in which the word occurs. We may note that his ability to give a similar account of the meaning scheme of a grammatical form or an intonation or stress pattern is probably much less. This does not, however, prevent him from using these purposefully or understanding them when he hears them in a situation. The ability to *talk about* the situations in which certain bits of language occur is apparently confined for most people to vocabulary or complete utterances; hence the popular notion that only words have meaning.

So far we have established that for language to be meaningful the speaker must be acting in some sort of recognisable relationship to his environment, and for a listener to understand what is said he must be aware of this relationship. But for this notion of meaning to be useful in teaching the semantic skill, we must look further into what the main features of a contextual situation are.

Clearly, at least two participants are involved (for we can ignore the situation of a person speaking to himself), the speaker and the hearer or hearers; the eavesdropper is not part of the situation.

Now, a great deal of language is meaningful only in terms of the two participants and their verbal behaviour. Imagine two elderly gentlemen chatting about their schooldays forty years earlier. There is nothing which happens around them—the traffic, the pneumatic drills, the weather—nor in their physical surroundings, which might be a public bar, the top of a bus or a bench in the park, which can help to make their conversation meaningful to an eavesdropper. Such language is the most difficult to explain because what is relevant in the situation—the family history, the education, social background, attitudes and temperament of the speaker and his listener—is not immediately apparent and indeed may remain permanently hidden.

But take the contrasting example of two men co-operating in some practical task, like laying drainpipes; every bit of language can probably be readily related to what they are doing, what is happening around them and what they are saying. Here the

20

relevant features of the situation are public, and although the characters of the participants play a part in determining the language it is largely at the formal level that it will happen, and even an eavesdropper would have little difficulty in understanding everything they said.

We are now in a position to state the main categories of situational features which are relevant for an understanding of meaning. They are, firstly, the participants in the situation, the speaker and hearer or hearers; then the actions of the participants occurring before or after the piece of language we want to understand. These actions may, of course, be verbal or non-verbal. Thus, a question is a question because it is habitually followed by the verbal action, on the part of the listener, which we call answer, not, we may note, because of its linguistic form which may or may not be interrogative. Similarly an order is an order because it is habitually followed by obedient action on the part of the listener, not because it has an imperative form. It should cause no surprise that actions in a situation, relevant for an understanding of a bit of language, can as well occur after as before it, for, after all, an eavesdropper often only understands what has been said as a result of what someone else proceeds to do or say.

But if someone says to you: 'Did you hear that?' it is evident he is making a response not to something you said or did, but more likely to an event for which neither of you was responsible. Clearly, events outside the control of the participants may be relevant for an understanding of an utterance. And if events can be relevant so can other circumstances—physical environment of the participants, the furniture, the buildings, the countryside and so on. These have been mentioned last because, contrary perhaps to expectation, they are undoubtedly the least important category of relevant features in most contextual situations.

Between the two examples we gave of the elderly gentlemen talking together, where the participants were only relevant features, to the workmen laying a drain, where the participants were the least important features, we find every possible intermediate sort of contextual situation.

For teaching meaning, however, the most useful contextual situations are those in which understanding depends largely on relevant features which can be recognised immediately by the learner, and thus used to give meaning to the language being taught. But more will be said about this in the next chapter.

Section III The Teaching of Meaning

The teaching of the formal meaning of language is the development of the learner's organisational skills, the ability to generate and analyse linguistic structures, whether they have to do with patterns of sound, of grammatical units, or with patterns of words. The procedures we use to teach these are familiar: drills of all sorts, substitution, completion and conversion exercises, spelling practice, ear training and so on. But when we have succeeded in teaching a measure of organisational skill we still have to show the learner when to use the forms he is able to create, in what circumstances the forms become effective in communication; in short, we have to teach him semantic skill, how to make use of the language meaningfully.

To a large extent, of course, the teaching of the organisational skills and the semantic skill proceed simultaneously. We have already noted that there would be no reason for teaching the one without the other; to do so led to verbalism.

There are three ways of teaching situational meaning; this is how Bloomfield describes them:

One is *demonstration*. If someone did not know the meaning of the word *apple*, we could instruct him by handing him an apple or pointing at an apple, and continuing as long as he made mistakes, to handle apples and point at them, until he used the word in the conventional way. This is essentially the process by which children learn the use of speech-forms. If a questioner understood enough of our language, we could define the word *apple* for him by *circumlocution*—that is, in the manner of our dictionaries, by roundabout speech which fitted the same situation as does the word *apple*, saying, for instance: 'The well-known, firm-fleshed, smooth-skinned round or oblong pome fruit of the tree of the genus Malus, varying greatly in size, shape colour and degree of acidity.' Or else, if we knew enough of the questioner's language, we could answer him by *translation*— that is by uttering a roughly equivalent form of his language; if he were a Frenchman, for instance, we could give *pomme* as the meaning of *apple*. This method of definition appears in our bilingual dictionaries.[1]

These three ways of giving, or teaching, meaning will be called *situational contextualisation*, *description* and *translation* in this book, and we shall examine each in turn, starting with the last.

This is not the place to go into the problem of translation in detail, although an understanding of the processes involved will help to a better assessment of its value in the teaching of languages. What we are concerned with here is whether we can leave all, or indeed any part, of the teaching of situational meaning and the development of the semantic skill to translation. Let us first remind ourselves that this was traditionally the *only* teaching of meaning, and it was specifically against this aspect of language teaching that the Direct Method was developed many years ago now. Teachers must then, as they do now, have felt that translation was not the only or the best way of developing semantic skill.

When we attempt to teach meaning by means of translation what we are, in fact, doing is to put the listener into the position of having to make an assumption about the bit of language we are teaching, which may be more or less false. He has no alternative to doing so because the teacher provides his only experience of the language or source of information about it. He will assume that the piece of language translated behaves in the language he is learning in an identical way to that in which it behaves in his mother-tongue. Now this can be regarded as a process of generalisation from one particular instance, which is, as we all know, liable to result in mistaken conclusions. Unfortunately sometimes the teacher actually encourages this process by making a generalised statement of meaning himself.

Instead of saying: '*In this sentence "la cabeza" means "head"*', he says, ' *"La cabeza" means "head"* '. The first statement may well be

[1] L. Bloomfield: op. cit.

true, while the second is demonstrably false; the most common translation of these words in Spanish do not incorporate *cabeza* anywhere in their formation: *headstone, headmaster, headgear, headway*. Here is what C. C. Fries has to say on this subject:

> Many people naïvely assume that the 'words' of diverse languages are simply different sets of symbols for the same things. Many people assume not only that a language consists solely of words that can be recorded and defined in a dictionary, but also that each word refers to some fact of reality about which every individual has had essentially the same experience. From this point of view all that is necessary for the mastery of a second language is to learn a new name for each particular item. If one could only memorise these names he would, they believe, have at once an ability of expression in the second language equivalent to that which he has in his native language.[1]

In any case the unit of situational meaning is the utterance; it therefore stands to reason that if we really wish to use translation as a means of showing meaning, we should never translate any stretch of language shorter than a sentence. This is rarely the use to which we put translation in the classroom. Much more often translation is used to 'give the meaning' of a single word. Thus we may say *conocer* means *to know*; or of a tense of grammar; *il est revenu à deux heures* means *he came back at two*; or of an intonational pattern: *il est revenu?* with a rising tone means *has he come back?*

In the first instance the English item *to know* is used with facts, historical, scientific and so on, *as well as* with the names of people, places, etc. But the Spanish word occurs *only* with the names of people and places, etc. Therefore, *to know* sometimes 'means' the same thing and sometimes it doesn't. In the second example the tense in French, *passé composé*, occurs together with an adverbial of definite past time. So does the English past tense. But the French tense *also* occurs with *encore*: *il n'est pas revenu encore*, where

[1] Charles C. Fries: *Teaching and Learning English as a Foreign Language*, University of Michigan Press, Ann Arbor, 1954.

the translation, *he didn't come back yet* is not normal in British English.[1]

Finally, whilst a rising tone does mean a question in French, any teacher knows that a yes-no question may or may not have a rising tone in English. This depends on a number of other circumstances.

The second method of teaching meaning—by description of the contextual situation in which the item occurs—suffers from two main weaknesses: firstly, that it is almost impossible to give a correct or complete description, and secondly, that talking about a skill is an inefficient way of teaching it.

Is it a realistic aim to try to describe the situation in which a single form, let alone a complete utterance, will occur? Besides, which language are we going to do our describing in? It would be a pity to do it in the pupil's own language, since it takes up valuable time better spent on exposing him to the language he is meant to be studying. On the other hand he cannot usually be expected to know enough to understand a description in the language he is learning.

This way of teaching meaning is that of the monolingual dictionary. It is also the technique of many grammars for foreign learners:

§ 31. *May* is a defective verb having neither infinitive nor participles. It has the past tense *might*.

May is used to express:

(a) Permission. E.g. You may go out when you have finished your work.

May I use your dictionary?

(b) Doubt, Uncertainty. E.g. He may arrive at the station in time if he hurries.

He may not have done it.

(c) Possibility. In this case *may* is used in the affirmative but not in the negative or interrogative. E.g. You may lead a horse to water but you cannot make him drink. (Note that

[1] It is, however, normal in American English. The American past tense and the British past tense therefore *mean* different things. Note, incidentally, that I have assumed for argument that *encore* and *yet* mean the same thing.

although *may* is used in the first part of the sentence, *can* is used in the second part, which is negative.)
Compare:

May I swim? (Have I your permission?)
Can he swim? (Does he know how to?)[1]

It is also the technique which is now being extended to features of pronunciation, such as intonation, as in this example:

Tone III This tone is used on statements and requests, but hardly ever on questions. It always gives the impression that something has been left unsaid, and that the speaker expects his hearer to imagine the extra meaning—in other words it is an implicatory tone. The implication is sometimes that the speaker hesitates to make his statement too confidently, and at other times it conveys a warning or (especially in the low variety) an apology.[2]

Now, books of this sort undoubtedly have a great deal of interesting *information* in them, and perhaps they may serve as a means of checking whether a learner has used a form to convey the meaning he intended. But it is difficult to see how they can be used to develop the semantic skill. A learner has no time to analyse the situation *consciously* when he is speaking. He cannot say 'Now let me see: am I dealing with a situation which is possible rather than uncertain, if so, is the word I want *can* or *may*?' Nor can he consider whether he ought to hesitate to make his statement too confidently and employ Tone III.

This is teaching the semantic skill by means of information, as it was called in Chapter II, and though, as has been suggested, it has a place in language teaching, it suffers from the same disadvantages that teaching by information does in the content subjects, that of producing verbalism. Our pupils may be able to give us a good account of when they ought to use, say, the present perfect tense, and yet rarely use it in the right situation in practice. This is teaching language by talking *about* it.

[1] A. S. Hornby: *Composition Exercises in Elementary English*, Macmillan, 1942.
[2] Roger Kingdon: *English Intonation Practice*, Longmans, 1958.

The third way of teaching meaning is by showing the language, never in units less than a complete utterance, occurring in real or simulated situations. This we called *contextualisation*, and it is the way we learn the semantic skill in our own language. Only at a later and more formal stage in learning our mother-tongue do we have resort to learning meaning by description and then largely of vocabulary.

The process is inevitably a slow one, but it is reasonably sure and undoubtedly effective. Over many years we observe the relationships which all the components of our language enter into in contexts of situation. In this way we build up for ourselves very slowly the situational meaning of those elements, whether they are bits of grammar, vocabulary or patterns of pronunciation. We never learn the 'whole' meaning of anything, even in our own language, if indeed there is any useful sense in which we can talk about the whole meaning of any bit of language.

Learning meaning this way is, it must be admitted, a slow process. But if it is a slow process in the mother-tongue how can we expect it to be anything else in the second language? We cannot therefore reasonably expect a learner to get the meaning of a word[1] or a piece of grammar after only a few demonstrations of its occurrence in a contextual situation. But then we know we cannot achieve the learning of meaning any quicker by description or translation, however attractive the latter may appear superficially. It only takes a second to give a translation, but we should be fools if we thought that the meaning had been *learnt* in a second also!

The fact is that the learner needs time to learn the meaning of a bit of language, just as we do in our mother-tongue. He will in any case only learn *some* of its meaning. But that doesn't matter. If we do our job as teachers we shall put him in the way of learning *enough* of its meaning for the purpose for which he is likely to need it. But at least we shall not have misled him, as we should have done, however unwittingly, by using translation; or confuse him, as we certainly should have done, by using description.

If, then, the best way of teaching meaning is the presentation of

[1] This is not true of 'words of unique reference' such as the names of people or places or the scientific names of substances, plants and animals.

the language to be taught in situational contexts, so that the learner may observe the relationships that exist between language and situation, then we have to do with the process of *teaching through the senses* instead of teaching through language itself, i.e. through information.

The relevant elements of a context of situation are perceived through the senses—any of the senses. Most obviously, the verbal element of the situation is perceived through the sense of hearing (or sight in the case of written language), but the other relevant features of the situation—the participants and what they do, and the physical circumstances of the situation—street, room, bus, etc., and what is happening in them, are noted predominantly *by the sense of sight.* The senses of touch and smell and the sense of taste, play a far smaller part in building up a meaning-giving picture of the situational context than the senses of sight and hearing. The teaching of words like *rough, smooth, sour, sweet, taste* and *smell,* which have to do with situational features perceived through the 'minor' senses, can be taught through their *formal* meaning alone, that is, through association with the words they normally occur with: *rough—sea, road; sweet—sugar, honey; sour—lemon, acid; smell—scent, flowers, smoke,* and so on, but would normally be taught through the senses of smell, taste and touch.

As in learning generally through the senses, the sense of sight is dominant. We cannot expect to build up the contextual relationships out of which meaning arises without depending almost entirely upon *visual means* of doing so. This is what is meant by the *visual element in language teaching.*

We can exemplify this notion by taking two or three very common procedures in language teaching. When we hold up or point to an object and say: '*This is a pencil*', we are reproducing a classroom variant of a situation which occurs frequently outside. This situation is sometimes called a *demonstration situation* and one of its verbal features is language of this sort: *this is a . . .* or, *that is a . . .* Another feature of a demonstration situation is pointing movements on the part of the speaker and the use of a particular word *only* when a particular physical feature of the situation is present. Thus we do not go around saying *this is a pencil* when there are no visible pencils in the situation. This does not mean that we don't talk about pencils when pencils are not present; only that we do not use the grammatical form: *this is a* . . . in those circumstances.

This is a theoretically more correct way of saying that, when we say: *this is a pencil* and point to something, the 'name' of the object we point to is *pencil*. What we are doing by this technique is creating a relationship between a sentence: *this is a pencil*, and all the features of situational context not just the pencil. This used to be known as the learning of meaning by direct association, and the method, as we know, got the name of the Direct Method. In it we were said to be creating a direct, meaningful association between an object and its name. This is partially true. Not everyone who favoured the Direct Method seemed to be aware that this could only happen in the presence of a demonstration-type situation characterised by the grammatical structure: *this is* . . . and accompanied by a characteristic movement by the teacher. In the absence of both these necessary conditions no association would take place and no learning of meaning result. If the teacher put his hands in his pockets and said: *pencil*, the pupils would never learn the 'meaning' of the word *pencil*.

It is evident from this explanation that such a technique of teaching meaning could not be used in the dark or over radio or gramophone. It is exclusively a visual technique.

Much of the teaching of vocabulary, in the earlier stages at least, is of this sort and is possible because the situational meaning of words like *pencil* or *blackboard* is relatively simple. But in the later stages we have to teach language in which the situational meaning is more complex, that is, in which the relationship between item and features of the situational context is not so direct. In this case we are normally thrown back on teaching the *formal* meaning of the items. How often, even in reading our own language, we meet words whose meaning we don't know, and yet by the end of the chapter or book we understand them. Teachers too often encourage pupils to use a dictionary unnecessarily ('meaning by description') when, by reading on, they will learn the meaning from the formal context.

This discussion of the teaching of the situational meaning of a word can be paralleled by the teaching of the meaning of some grammatical structures. The meaning of the *imperative* is normally taught by giving an order which is *seen* to be obeyed. The teaching of the first tenses—continuous present, present perfect and future—is usually done by situational teaching. But as with the more difficult vocabulary items, we tend to fall back in the case of the more 'difficult' tenses, upon teaching their formal meaning, for example, the sequence of tenses in conditional sentences: it *would have been* impossible, if he *had not helped*.

It is not always easy to devise a technique of presentation which gives meaning to a single constituent element such as a word or an idiom, a tense or a mood. The meaning of such things emerges rather out of a number of contextualisations of complete utterances. Language items less than a complete sentence cannot be individually contextualised, since only complete utterances occur in normal speech situations. Even an utterance consisting of only one word, like *Go!* is linguistically several different items. It is a sentence in grammar; it is an imperative verb form; it is a vocabulary word; and it has a characteristic intonation pattern. All these things are taught simultaneously when we teach it situationally. Hence the value of situational teaching at all stages. Although we may have a particular bit of language—a point of grammar or pronunciation or a bit of vocabulary—in focus at any moment, the linguistic context of the whole utterance is being re-presented or revised, and its meaning re-taught. This is also why we are careful to introduce new bits of language in the context of what is already familiar. The new item gets its meaning *formally* from the linguistic context and situationally from the situational context.

Situational teaching, however, is not the only means we have of giving situational meaning. If we were confined to the situational material that the classroom offered, we should soon have exhausted all the possibilities of this method of teaching. Two further contextualising techniques are available: first, dramatisation, and second, the introduction into the classroom of representations of contextualised language through film-strips, film and television. We can also introduce pictures. These are the equivalent of the window as a visual aid, for when we talk about a picture we have escaped from the classroom situation although we still teach situationally.

We must be careful to note that radio, gramophone and tape recordings, being solely concerned with the sense of hearing, cannot teach situational meaning. Their powers of contextualisation are limited to 'sound-effects'—dogs barking, noises of traffic, trains and aeroplanes and the like. Hence the *very* heavy dependence (when these methods are used alone) on translation, verbal description of meaning, and the illustrations in the Student's Book.

But we have now mentioned pictures, film, film-strips, television, and these, being associated with visual techniques of teaching, are the subject of the next chapter.

3
The Visual Element in Language Teaching

Section I Visual Materials

The techniques of teaching meaning outlined in the previous chapter involved making use of the situation in which the pupil and teacher find themselves in order to give meaning to the language being taught. Such teaching is called situational teaching; but it is immediately evident that if we were to rely solely on what is available in any ordinary classroom as potential elements in a situational context, we could not progress beyond a certain point in our teaching without having recourse to translation, description or teaching through formal meaning alone. This is where a consideration of visual materials comes in.

Anything that the learner can see in the classroom or through the window is potentially a visual element in the teaching of meaning. This applies to the permanent fittings of the classroom such as walls, doors and windows; to its usual furnishings, desks, cupboards, chairs, blackboards and bookshelves; to things which are introduced into it either normally, such as books or writing materials, or abnormally, such as animals, plants and tools; or indeed anything in the world which is transportable and small enough to be got through the door.

None of these things so far mentioned are usually called visual aids, and yet in most language teaching situations they are more important than those materials usually called by that name.

The list so far has consisted only of physical objects but we already know that these represent only one element in a context of situation and by no means the most important. We must add, then, to the list of potential visual materials any person in sight of the learner, whether pupil or teacher, or anyone else who can be persuaded to visit the classroom. These are the potential participants in the context of situation. They too could, with equal justice, be called visual aids; even audio-visual aids, since they talk. Thus, without any doubt, the teacher is the most important audio-visual aid to learning in the classroom.

But this is still not the whole story. Anything that can be seen to happen in the classroom is equally a potential visual element of the context. It is very often the sign of an alert teacher that he can turn a chance and unplanned event to good account. I well recall a teacher in training who, while demonstrating visually '*getting up*' and '*getting down*', jumped on to a chair with such force that it broke and spilled him onto the floor. Like a flash he started: '*This chair is broken*', '*It was not very strong*', '*If I jump on that one will it break?*' and so on.

There are many things in the world which cannot be brought into the classroom, such as elephants, pyramids and atom bombs; there are many people who do not normally come into the classroom: bank managers, cabinet ministers and cowboys; and even more obviously, there are many things which cannot happen in a classroom; a surgical operation, catching a bus and swimming the Channel.

If we had no way whatsoever of introducing such things, people and events into the classroom we should have to fall back upon teaching the language associated with them by translation and description, or (and this would be the best alternative) by simulation of the situations in which these things happened; that is, by dramatisation.

We can act an operation, cowboys and elephants. When we do this we re-create in our imaginations the context of situation in which these things belong. But to do so we have to call upon a more or less developed knowledge of his environment such as was assumed in the learner in the introduction to this book. Obviously we shall achieve little if we introduce situational elements into our contextualising procedures which are unknown or unfamiliar to the learner; strange, unknown situational features can scarcely be used to give meaning to language.

Besides simulation, we have other means of introducing these things into the classroom. For this purpose we use representational visual material specially prepared for the teaching of the language belonging say, to surgical operations, catching buses and swimming the Channel. These materials—drawings, photographs, models, diagrams presented on charts, on film strips, cine films or on TV—are what are normally thought of as visual or audio-visual aids.

These so-called aids now fall into perspective when considered in this way alongside the great variety and extent of the 'real' and 'simulated' visual experience which we can make use of in the classroom to give meaning to the linguistic forms we teach, i.e. to develop the semantic skill. In language teaching anything visible can be used by the teacher to teach meaning. It is an arbitrary division of the wealth of visual materials available to the teacher to call some 'aids' and not others. It leads most often to the teacher's failure to make good use of what is immediately to hand in favour of expensive and often not particularly appropriate imported material. It leads to that height of absurdity which one sometimes meets: a wall-chart drawing of a classroom full of pupils being used by a teacher to teach the language of the classroom.

We can see already that we have a variety of criteria available for the classification of the visual materials for the teaching of meaning:

a Real things, people and events normally present in the classroom.

b Real things, people or events specially introduced into the classroom for the language lesson.

c Simulated or pictorially represented things, people and events.

d Purely visual materials, materials which *may* be accompanied by language and materials which are always accompanied by language (audio-visual aids).

It can easily become an exercise in ingenuity to make further more refined classifications. Under pictorial representation, for example, we could list blackboard drawing, flannelgraph, plastigraph, magnetic boards, wall charts and photographs. This is the sort of classification and sub-classification which is frequently indulged in when discussing visual aids, and is based on the *medium* of representation. The artist classifies his material in this way: oil paints, water-colour, etching, lithograph, etc. What we have to ask ourselves here is which, if any, of these classifications has relevance to language teaching. In other words, does a photograph help to teach meaning in language in a different way from a drawing? The answer is obviously not.

As far as giving meaning to language is concerned, all materials function in the same way. That much was clear from the discussions in Chapter 2. But it may be that for certain purposes a drawing is more effective than a photograph. Indeed this will usually be so. This matter is dealt with in later sections. And, of course, it is certainly true that different techniques of teaching are involved in the use of real situations in contrast with simulated situations, or pictorially represented situations.

There is another way of classifying the visual materials we have been discussing and that is according to the *use* made of them by the learner. In this form of classification we are not concerned with the nature of the material itself in the first instance, that is, whether it is a thing to be handled, or a drawn or projected representation of something, but with what the learner does with it.

The learner may make use of what we have called visual materials for his normal everyday purposes—tools, pencils, knives, scissors, doors; these are things which he uses regularly outside the classroom, but he rarely *talks* about them. We could classify these visual materials as things which the learner uses for talking *with*. Language is an accompaniment to an activity in which these things have a part.

When children, for instance, are making a drawing, the teacher may talk with them about the paper, pencils, paints, brushes and colours they are using to make the picture. For the pupils *the picture* is the centre of attention; for the teacher, however, it is *the language* connected with picture-making. This type of situational teaching is the truest and most effective because the language used is completely and naturally contextualised, thus producing the most solid and rapid learning of meaning.

The second sort of material is for talking *about*. In everyday life we *use* pictures, films and television programmes, but they are the *object* of the activity itself and not an accessory. We use them for getting information, pleasure and recreation. And, of course, we do talk *about* them. But we do so *after* rather than *while* we are 'using' them and our discussions are critical rather than descriptive.

It is possible, of course, to talk *about* pencils, scissors, books and brushes. This is frequently done in the classroom. It is really a second-class sort of situational teaching because it is an activity peculiar to the classroom, even more so to the language classroom. In the world outside, people discuss films, pictures and television programmes, but they do not usually discuss pencils and handkerchiefs. They use them. The rather fatuous conversation of the type: 'Are you a boy or a girl?' and 'Is this knife made of stone or metal?' quickly loses its interest, because here language is the centre of interest for both teacher and pupil. In life outside the classroom language is rarely the centre of interest, and, except at the babbling and practice stage of mother-tongue learning, it is rarely indulged in for its own sake.[1] It is true that grammatical and lexical forms may need practice, that is, the formal meaning may require more teaching than the situational meaning, but in good situational teaching the teacher will find ways of giving the necessary practice in learning forms without resorting to these artificial procedures. When the teacher says, 'Is the man in the picture holding a rake or a spade?' the learner knows that the teacher knows the answer. He is therefore behaving unnaturally. This sort of language behaviour is not normally rewarding and does not therefore lead to good learning.

It is, however, important to note that the relative effectiveness of these procedures depends upon the age of the learner. Sophisticated adult learners are prepared to accept a great deal of 'abnormal' linguistic behaviour in the classroom because their motivation is a long term one. They see more clearly how such procedures may lead to learning a language skill. For them language *is* indeed the centre of attention, but for the younger child this is not so. He requires a more immediate reward for his

[1] Unless one regards the writing and reading of 'Literature' as indulging in language for its own sake. See Halliday, MacIntosh & Strevens: *The Linguistic Sciences and Language Teaching*, Part V, Section 5, Longmans, 1964.

activities and for him language cannot usefully be the centre of attention for long.

To sum up, we use visual techniques in order to teach meaning; that is, to develop the semantic skill. But, as we saw, there are other skills to learn—organisational and motor-perceptive. The practice of these can, to a greater or lesser degree, go on without the activity being meaningful linguistically. But from the point of view of motivation for learning, the indulgence in what is really unnatural behaviour is liable to cause loss of interest, and boredom. Hence the insistence that the practice of organisational and motor-perceptive skills should take place through activities which are *otherwise* meaningful and rewarding, and regarded as 'sensible' by the young learner. The best situational teaching, including dramatic techniques, singing, dancing, making things, playing games and drawing, *is* meaningful activity in its own right, whilst grammar pattern drill and certain types of pronunciation practice and ear-training, in isolation, are not.

Section II Visual Materials and the Teacher

The teacher in the classroom rarely stands alone before his class. At his elbow, but invisible, stand perhaps several other unacknowledged teachers. As W. R. Lee says, 'Teaching is not a solitary enterprise, whatever the pupils may think, even if occasionally the teacher thinks likewise.'[1]

To a greater or lesser extent, and usually it is to a greater extent, the teacher is dependent upon his textbook. The man who wrote it probably knew more about his subject than the teacher, and he probably knew more about how to teach his subject. It is he who has chosen what is to be taught in the classroom and the order in which to teach it. He may even suggest how to teach it and in what situations. His, too, are many of the practice materials. For the most part teachers are only too glad to leave these matters to the 'invisible' teacher; after all, they have quite enough to do dealing directly with the learner.

So long as the teaching of most subjects was done largely

[1] W. R. Lee: 'Mass Media and the Pupil–Teacher Relationship,' *The Year Book of Education, 1960*, Evans, London, 1960.

through language, the only invisible teacher was the textbook writer or syllabus designer. But when visual methods began to come in, they brought with them other invisible teachers: the men who designed the wall charts, who prepared the film-strips, who wrote the scripts of the film or television lessons. And finally, to crown it all, they ceased to be invisible, because the face which appears on the TV screen belongs to one of them.

We are not here concerned with the effect that the admission of the invisible teachers into the classroom will have (or indeed has already had in some places) upon the relationship between teachers and pupils. This has been very well dealt with in the article by Dr. Lee, quoted above. That there is such an effect cannot now be doubted. What we are concerned with is the effect that the introduction of these visual materials into the classroom may have on the teacher's control over his materials and methods.

The teacher who has no invisible colleague at his elbow is assumed to be in entire control; he decides *what* to teach, *when* to teach it and *how* to present, practise and test it. In other words he makes his own selection of the teaching points, orders them into a syllabus and devises his own methodology and testing procedures. The teacher who relies on his invisible colleagues may hand over all or any of these responsibilities to him. He may accept the selection of material in the textbook but present it in a different order; he may accept both the selection and grading but teach the material in his own way. Alternatively he may carefully follow the suggestions on method in the teacher's handbook, and very often he leaves the testing to others. Most teachers accept help in one form or another—this is only right and proper, since few teachers have had that degree of training and experience which qualifies them to make all these decisions themselves. In particular they normally lack the linguistic training which permits them to make a competent selection of grammatical, pronunciation and vocabulary items for a course. Furthermore it is more economical of time and energy for some of these functions to be performed centrally.

We can consider the teacher's control over the visual materials in the same way. The teacher may make his own decisions on what materials to use, and when and how to use them, or he may hand over some of these decisions to the designer of those materials. This is even more understandable in that the skills of draughtsmanship, puppet-making, script-writing and photography, for example, are specialised and are probably not those which he has been trained in. The tendency towards mechanisation and the introduction of expensive equipment inevitably brings with it higher degrees of specialisation, and, as a result, the relationship between the teacher and his invisible colleague is increasingly similar to that of the general practitioner and the hospital doctor in the medical field. As in the case of the general practitioner, once he makes the decision to send his patient to hospital he loses control. Thus, in extreme cases, the teacher reserves only the right to decide *whether* to use the newer materials or not. Having decided to do so, he then has little further say in the matter. All he now does is to switch on the TV receiver, adjust the picture and the sound level, and then see that the children behave themselves.

Let us now, using the classification made in the last section, take some examples. The teacher has complete control over the visual materials, people and events which are natural to the classroom. In other words, situational teaching is wholly within the teacher's control and can be carried out only by him. Natural full contextualisation is entirely in his hands. By this we mean that the decision to use the foreign language as a medium of communication while carrying on such activities as painting, drawing, model-making, gymnastics or dancing—all normal classroom activities—is entirely his. So is the decision to use simulated contextualisation in the form of dramatisations, since neither of these require the importation into the classroom of specially produced visual or linguistic material.

The teacher also fully controls (if he has the necessary skill) the representational pictorial material that he may draw on the blackboard or which he may build up on the flannelgraph or plastigraph. It is when he begins to introduce into his classroom specially designed materials that he gradually hands over control to the invisible teacher. The admission of visual materials in the form of wall pictures, charts, maps, illustrations or photographs is the beginning. He may still decide *whether* to use them, and if so, *when* and *how* to use them; he can still use them in his own way, but the content of the material, that is, what is in the drawing, and, if a textbook illustration, which piece of text should be illustrated, is not in his hands, and consequently the meanings that will be taught by means of them must to some extent be out of his control. This is not perhaps a very serious matter. He does not, after all, choose texts or materials that do not fit his purpose, nor does he have to teach everything that the material was designed to teach. Nevertheless, it is improbable that material of this sort can ever be as specific to his purpose as the teacher's own drawings. It may, for example, contain contextual features which he would not himself have chosen, or at least not at that point in the course. He will then be inclined to modify the language he teaches to fit the pictorial material, rather than use the picture to teach the language he wishes. After all, the visual element is introduced to give meaning to the language, not the language to explain the picture. This was discussed in the Introduction.

The next stage is loss of control over the *method* of presentation. This is clearly seen in the introduction of sound film into the classroom. In the previous examples it was the teacher who presented the language to which the visual element gave meaning. Now the teacher no longer does this. The language element and the visual element are both in the hands of the invisible teacher. The process of contextualisation has been wholly handed over. The only control the teacher now exercises is in the decision *whether* he will use the materials and, if so, *when*; that is, at what point they will best fit into the total framework of the syllabus that he has adopted.

The last stage is when the teacher can no longer even decide *when* he wishes to use the audio-visual material. This stage is represented by the television lesson. At this point the invisible teacher becomes visible. He takes over the full responsibility, for the time being at least, for the teaching, while the classroom teacher acts as monitor, switching the set on and off and keeping order.

We often hear the cry that television cannot replace the teacher. It is both true and untrue. Television as a technical medium does not do away with *a* teacher. It may transpose him in space and time. He operates from the studio at a time which suits him and the TV station. He can take over much of the responsibility of the *classroom teacher.* He may even be able to teach in the absence of a classroom teacher, though this is doubtful. But if there is a well-qualified teacher in the classroom TV will not 'replace' him; it is more likely to 'free' him to do a better job, to concentrate on those things which he can do and the TV teacher cannot, and leave those things to the TV teacher which he can do better, such as contextualise language material more efficiently.

We can represent the material of this section graphically in this way:

VISUAL MATERIAL	CONTROL BY TEACHER		
	content	timing	method
1 Real things, people, events	✓	✓	✓
2 Blackboard drawings	✓	✓	✓
3 Dramatisation, puppetry	✓	✓	✓
4 Printed wall pictures, etc.	×	✓	✓
5 Film strips	×	✓	✓
6 Audio-visual courses	×	✓	×
7 Film	×	✓	×
8 TV programmes	×	×	×

Section III Relevant Features in Visual Materials

As we have seen, language is part and parcel of a context of situation. Firth, in the quotation given on page 16, insists upon this. In our everyday experience our understanding of what is going on in a situation in which language occurs is derived from the relationship between the language and the other relevant features of the situation. Remove the non-linguistic features of the situation and we no longer fully understand the language; or alternatively remove the language and we no longer fully understand what is going on. We illustrated this earlier on by reference to watching a television programme either without the sound or without the vision.

The conclusions we must draw from these facts are that in teaching anything, subject or language, we must be on our guard against making the assumption that our pupils understand. We must not take it for granted that they have enough language to understand our explanations of the subject, or vice versa, that they have enough knowledge of the world to understand the language. In short, we must be quite sure in language teaching that our pupils *understand what they see* of the visual element of the situational context; that is, they must not only see what the teacher intends them to see, but also recognise it for what it is and understand its relationship with the other features. They must do this so quickly and so completely that the language they are being taught is immediately filled with meaning.

An equivalent process goes on in the understanding of an illustrated joke such as may be found in *Punch*. There are some jokes one 'sees' immediately; there are others one has to study in order to 'get' the point, and there are some which one never 'gets' because one has not discerned the relevant features in the picture and related them to the caption. Here is an example taken from *Punch*:

'*Well, here we go again.*'

It would be interesting to know how many readers 'saw' the point in this joke. Possibly none. It was, in fact, published just before

Christmas and the following words occurred at the top of the page: *PUNCH, December 26, 1962.* This one additional fact—the date of publication—is a *relevant feature* of the context of situation in which the joke was to be understood. Without it there could at best be only a doubtful understanding of what it was all about.

The efficient use of visual material depends upon the recognition of what the *relevant visual features* of the situation are that give meaning to the language being presented. Thus, to refer back to the example in Chapter 2, it is necessary when teaching the meaning of *pencil* by saying '*This is a pencil*' that the pencil itself should be visible and that the teacher should be seen to be pointing to, or otherwise clearly indicating, the pencil. The *relevant features* of this demonstration situation are *the object*: the pencil; *the action*: pointing to a pencil, which must be near to the participant, and *the language*: '*This is a pencil*'. Any deviation from the relevant features will make comprehension more uncertain or even impossible. This example is one of the utmost simplicity, and this is, of course, why the demonstration technique is used so much in the earlier stages of a language course.

The relevant visual features of most contextual situations are more numerous and their interrelations more subtle. It is, nevertheless, part of the teacher's job to be able to distinguish the features which are relevant from those which are not. An instructive technique is to take any illustrated joke and try to identify the features.

'*Pardon, Monsieur . . . veuillez m'indiquer la route pour Dover?*'

Why should the motorist address the obviously English householder in French? Let us now restore one item which had been
removed from the original illustration.

'*Pardon, Monsieur . . . veuillez m'indiquer la route pour Dover?*'

It certainly seems more understandable now that we know the
motorist was a Frenchman, but still it is not particularly funny. In
the next version we have reproduced the original illustration as it
was published.

'*Pardon, Monsieur . . . veuillez m'indiquer la route pour Dover?*'

Only now can we see where the joke lies. But even now there are
assumptions of knowledge in the reader. A relevant feature is that
the householder must be known to be English. This might not be

immediately apparent to someone who did not know that the English are in the habit of giving their houses names, and, furthermore, sometimes affect foreign names for the purpose, such as *Mon Repos* or, as here, *Chez Nous*.

The ability to pick out the relevant features of the situation and discern the relationships between them is dependent upon several factors. It depends upon the maturity and experience of the learner. He cannot be expected to spot features which are unknown to him, or which lie outside the range of his experience. He may be too young to understand, or he may be too unsophisticated. On the other hand, his failure to spot the relevance of the feature may be due to his social or cultural background. Daffodils do not grow in West Africa, nor breadfruit in Europe. Mothers-in-law have quite different relationships with their sons and daughters-in-law in different societies. The English mother-in-law jokes are not everywhere exportable. Finally, ability to pick out the relevant features of a situation may be affected by personal character traits such as attitudes, prejudices and interests. We see, therefore, what we understand, but we also see only what we are prepared or want to see. These are matters dealt with in the next section. All we need to note here is that the visual techniques and materials used in the classroom should be adapted to the capacities, education and social and geographic backgrounds of the learner. If they are not, the language they are meant to give meaning to will not be understood.

In discussing the relevant features of a situation, it seems wise to make a distinction between that type of situation, such as the ordinary classroom situation, in which the teacher has control over all the elements, including the language, and those simulated situations produced by the use of audio-visual materials, such as film, and television in which the teacher has control over neither the language nor the visual element of the context.

If the teacher has this control, he can see to it that all the relevant features are seen and understood; he knows the age, intelligence and cultural background of his pupils. In any case, in situational teaching, the pupils and teacher are themselves relevant features of the context, and the language, being a product of their interaction with each other and their physical

45

surroundings, is more readily understood. Furthermore, if understanding should not take place, the teacher has the means to
repeat the teaching and thus retrieve the situation.

On the other hand, where visual material and language come
as a single imported unit in which the pupil is not so clearly an
element in the situational context of the language, there is little
the teacher can do to make good failures in understanding except
by having recourse to translation and description. In the case of
such materials, therefore, the responsibility for ensuring that
understanding will take place is that of the invisible teacher.

The invisible teacher clearly has a much more difficult job in
the preparation of his audio-visual materials than the classroom
teacher. He must see that the language he is teaching is integral
with its visual context, and his problems in doing this arise from
the fact that he must start from the linguistic element and then
build it into a visual contextual situation, whilst the classroom
teacher, in situational teaching, starts with the contextual features
—people, events and things in the classroom—and allows his
language to arise out of them. The invisible teacher's first problem
is that he does not know his pupils in the way that their classroom
teacher does. For this reason he is more likely to make assumptions
about their knowledge and social and cultural background which,
if proved incorrect, may result in the learner's failing to understand his material. Secondly, in moving from language to visual
context, he is faced with the fact that we still know far too little
about the relationships between the features of context and those
of language to create unequivocally meaningful material. If our
knowledge were more developed, we should be able to give a
visual presentation of a context from which the learner could
predict the language which belonged to it with a high degree of
certainty. The experiments conducted by the Centre Audio-
Visuel de l'ENS de Saint-Cloud have shown that we are far from
being able to do this.[1]

It is true that we are capable of writing the dialogues for short

[1] G. Mialeret and C. Malandain: 'La perception du Film Fixe Chez L'Enfant'
in *Etudes de Linguistique Appliquée*, Didier, Paris, 1962. Also *Recherche sur la Com-
préhension du Film Fixe*, C.R.E.D.I.F., Ministère de L'Education Nationale,
1961 (cyclostyled).

speech episodes which a native speaker will accept as being 'realistic', that is, which he can imagine happening. But to go on from there to predict what the features, visual or otherwise, of the situational context will be for any particular utterance is still far beyond our knowledge. The best we can do at present is to proceed by trial and error.

Section IV Seeing, Recognising and Understanding Visual Material

Even if we were clever enough always to select those elements of the visual context which were relevant for teaching the meaning of a particular piece of language, we should not achieve our ends unless these features were *seen*, *recognised* and the whole picture *understood* by the learner.

We shall take each of these three requirements in turn and see what they imply.

The relevant features must be visible. This may seem an obvious requirement and yet it is quite common for the pupils simply not to see what they must see for understanding.

We must first know that the pupil's eyesight is adequate. And yet it is, alas, often discovered eventually that a pupil's poor progress in learning is due to his inability to see clearly, particularly what may be put on the blackboard.

It is the teacher's responsibility to see that *all* the pupils can see *all* the relevant features of the visual material. They must be visible all the time they are relevant. It is not sufficient for the learner to catch a fleeting glance of some object raised from the desk or taken out of the pocket. The object must be large enough for all to see, and that includes those sitting at the back of the classroom. It is unwise to make your teaching hang upon one paper-clip or one matchstick. If these are essential, then let every pupil have one. This is also true of actions, movements and gestures; all these must be visible and sufficiently prolonged to be noted by the learner. We must not have the pupils asking each other: 'What did he do?' or 'What is he doing?' The raising of an eyebrow or some other facial gesture may well be a relevant

feature of a situation. These can neither be enlarged nor prolonged, though they may perhaps be repeated. The pupils'
attention can certainly be directed to them. One must, however,
not fall into the practice of, say, prolonging an action until it
becomes ridiculous. You simply cannot *fall down* slowly. The
attempt to do so would be either funny or a different action. In
either case the meaning would be different and the object of the
operation defeated. Similarly one must be critical of such
practices, which are often thoughtlessly employed, as laboriously
opening and shutting doors, boxes, books and so on whilst
practising 'I am shutting (or opening) my book (the door)'. You
cannot open and shut a door both slowly and convincingly.

In using representational material, the drawings, pictures and
models must be *large* enough, and the detail in them which is
going to be relevant must be visible to the pupils farthest away.
Often the size of a picture is deceptive. The sheet on which it is
printed seems enormous and unwieldy, and yet when it comes to
using it the detail is still too small for all the learners to see. In the
case of TV one must not assign too many pupils to any one
receiver.

The picture must be *clear* enough. This obviously has to do with
size, but also with other qualities. Each detail must be separated
clearly from the next. This result is achieved by strong outlines,
or by good, distinctive colouring or by strong tonal contrast, and,
of course, in the case of projected material, correct focus.

Finally, the pictures should be *well-lit*. The best picture is useless in the dark. It is equally useless if the surface is reflective and
the pupils see nothing but a piece of shiny blackboard or paper on
the wall. Projected pictures must be powerfully enough lit in
relation to the amount of light naturally present in the room. TV
receivers may require a hood to avoid reflection and be placed in
the correct position in relation to windows and other sources of
light.

Secondly, what is relevant in the picture or situation must not
be outweighed or obscured by what is irrelevant. This is the
strongest argument in favour of material prepared by the teacher
for the teaching of a particular bit of language, against material
which it is hoped by the maker or publisher can be used for a

whole range of teaching jobs. Such material is likely to be cluttered up with so much 'information' that the relevant features for the teaching of a specific point are always to some degree obscured.

Relevant movements and actions in the classroom should, similarly, not be obscured by irrelevant simultaneously occurring action. This is most likely to happen where several people are engaged in building up a meaningful contextual situation. It is also particularly difficult to avoid in film material and even in the pictorial element in audio-visual courses.

The ways of overcoming the obscuring effect of irrelevant detail are twofold: the process of *simplification* in representation which will be dealt with later, and the method of *directing attention*.

This brings us again to the important point of *attention*. We see what we want to see; we readily overlook what we do not like or do not immediately understand or recognise. This is what is meant by the term 'psychological set'. 'Set' is a mental prepared-ness for something, whether perception or activity of other sorts.

Because something is physically in view is no assurance that it will be 'seen'. We are all familiar with the fact that when we are looking for something we have lost, it is all too easy to 'not see' it when it is under our nose. Therefore the teacher will, when the material is within his control, draw the learner's *attention* to the relevant features. This he may do by gesture, by lighting, or, of course, by language. This last way offers valuable opportunity for reteaching old material.

Relevant features must be *recognised*. It is not sufficient for them simply to be in the field of vision or even to be noted. They must also be recognised for what they are. This is the first step to under-standing. There are, however, a number of impediments to recognition. What the learner sees of the relevant features may not be presented to him in the form in which he is accustomed to seeing them. This is particularly liable to be the case with material presented on TV or film. In these media the producer has the power to make viewers look at things from the producer's point of view. It is obviously important, therefore, that in educational TV or film the producer should have an understanding of the problems which are discussed in this section, that he should have a 'learner's eye'. Thus, for example, a building viewed from above is not necessarily recognisable as such by younger children. The way a teacher performs an action, or the TV producer lets us see him do so, may not be the way a child has seen it done at home; the things in a picture may have a different colour or shape from the examples the learner has met before. In short, we can never take it for granted that what we present is immediately recognised.

This danger exists acutely in the materials we often have to use for language teaching. A language is, after all, an expression, to a greater or lesser degree, of the culture of its speakers. Thus there may easily be things, people and modes of behaviour which are totally unknown to the learner and therefore useless for giving meaning to the language being taught; these things may be known to him only through *information* in his mother-tongue but not through his direct sensory experience. This would be true, for example, of snow and ice, skating and ski-ing in many parts of Africa; or they may be known to him in a different form. Thus, for example, all countries have policemen, but the uniform they wear is different in every case. It would not always be easy for a learner to differentiate between a policeman, a soldier and a postman in all cases.

Cultural background can affect recognition in other ways, although this is probably becoming less so under the influence of the mass media of communication. Let us remember that two-dimensional representation is an abstraction, and, although practically all cultures have used pictorial representation, children have to learn to recognise what is depicted. In European culture, of course, this is done at a rather early age. Indeed, the time gap between learning *about* a thing and meeting pictorial representations of it may be very short indeed. This is nowadays probably more so than ever, to the extent that quite young children may learn about something from pictures first and then have to learn to recognise the object itself all over again.

But what is not always realised is that pictorial representation has certain conventions of abstraction which are accepted within certain cultures though not necessarily in others. If the artist who makes the visual material follows conventions different from those of the learner's culture, the understanding of the picture is delayed. 'Realism' may only mean that the style of representation follows accepted conventions. Many people reject modern art simply because it does not follow the traditional conventions of representation. This is not only, or necessarily, a question of the degree of abstraction. A child's picture of a mug (a) cannot be called more abstract or less realistic than that of the artist who follows the conventions of perspective to which Europeans, at least, have become conditioned (b)

(a)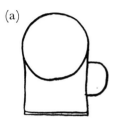

(b)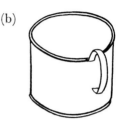

The child 'knows', i.e. has sensory experience of the fact, that the top of a mug is round, so he draws it so. Indeed this type of 'conceptual' drawing could be considered *more* realistic for this reason. It may well be that children of a certain age can recognise a cup drawn as in (a) more readily than that drawn in (b), because they have not yet been 'taught' the conventions of perspective.

The discussion which goes on about the desirability of a certain style or a certain degree of abstraction in the visual material used in the language teaching classroom is thus seen to resolve itself into two clearly defined questions:

  i Does the style of the illustration represent a degree of abstraction conventional in the culture of the learner?

  ii Do the style and degree of abstraction emphasise or obscure the relevant features for teaching?

A particular style and degree of abstraction in pictorial visual materials can be justified only if they serve to make the picture more readily understood, that is, if they highlight the relevant features without going against the pictorial conventions of the culture of the learner.

This would mean that, although the degree of abstraction represented by the use of pin-men illustration may be accepted

EDINBURGH UNIVERSITY LIBRARY
WITHDRAWN

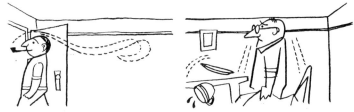

He walked *out* of the room   The cup fell *off* the table

CARICATURE

STYLISED

FLAT PATTERN

PIN-MEN WITH FACIAL EXPRESSIONS

by the culture of the learner, it would be no use employing them when such emotions as anger, remorse or disappointment were relevant features of the situational context, because the most important visual feature of these is facial expression, and this may be abstracted out in this style of drawing. On the other hand, if the learners did not 'understand' the abstraction of the pin-men in the first place, it would also be no use employing pin-men to illustrate, say, sawing up a log, although the relevant features of this activity can readily be shown by this technique.

We can now relate the notion of *abstraction* to that of *simplification* mentioned on page 49. All abstractions are simplifications, but the simplifications we are interested in are those which give prominence to what is *relevant* for teaching at the expense of what is *irrelevant*. The stylistic abstraction in itself is not necessarily concerned with the teaching properties of the picture. We must, therefore, be sure that abstraction serves our purpose as well as the artist's. On page 52 are some illustrations.

We have spoken so far only of the conventions of pictorial representation, but film and television similarly have conventions which the learner has to learn. Enough studies have now been made of the understanding of film to show that this is an important consideration. The director of a film or TV programme uses certain conventional techniques because he knows that the viewers have come to understand what they mean. If these conventions were to be disregarded then the viewer would be liable not to understand, to misunderstand or to understand too slowly. Thus, for example, when the TV director wants to show two people speaking to each other on the telephone, he sees to it that each faces out of the screen in the opposite direction.

You can well see that if we cut between this pair of shots the two people will not appear to be speaking to each other, whereas, if we reverse one of them, they will. Thus:

53

In the first example it would not be immediately apparent to the viewer that the characters were speaking to one another.[1] This is nothing more than a convention since, of course, in real life, when speaking *on the telephone* there is no reason why the speakers should look in any particular direction in relation to each other.

Finally, there is one more type of convention which is nowadays

I haven't any money   Which way is best

It's a four hours' walk   I can't see its number[2]

[1] This illustration comes from Desmond Davies: *The Grammar of Television Production*, Barrie and Rockliff, London, 1960.

[2] These are taken from Fontaine and Podeyn: *Direct Contact*, I.V.A.C., Belgium.

frequently used in visual materials for teaching: the use of symbols. A visual symbol is usually, but not always, an abstract form of pictorial representation, but there are, of course, visual symbols for things which have no physical existence. Negation, Interrogation, Distance, Choice, etc., are all concepts which are useful in visual materials in language teaching. But in using them we must be sure that these symbols are familiar to the learner in his own culture and that we have taught their meaning beforehand. In fact, many teachers and their classes develop a private symbology of their own.

| (d) Professeur: | Où vont elles? |
| Élève: | Elles vont prendre l'autobus. |

| Professeur: | Posez la question. |
| Élève: | À quelle heure part l'autobus. |

| Professeur: | Répondez. |
| Élève: | L'autobus part à cinq heures du matin. [1] |

This may even occur in live TV teaching where a movement of the hand or a turning of the head and inclining of the ear towards the viewer means: 'You repeat or practice now, I am listening', although the viewer knows perfectly well that the TV teacher cannot hear!

We have seen that the relevant features of the visual material must be *seen* and secondly, *recognised*. But for the material to be useful for teaching meaning in language it must also be *understood*.

Professor Vernon starts her chapter on the 'Perception of Special Types of Material' in her *Psychology of Perception*[2] with these words:

[1] Memory Aid Symbols from the Teaching Notes to the film *On Parle Français*, produced for the Department of Education and Science by Anvil Films in association with the Educational Foundation for Visual Aids.

[2] M. D. Vernon: *Psychology of Perception*, Penguin Books, 1962.

In the civilised state, man makes so much use of shapes drawn on flat surfaces that his ability to comprehend these has reached a high degree of efficiency. . . . But this capacity must be learnt, and the child only acquires it gradually, and sometimes only after much teaching.

Understanding what we see means perceiving relationships between the relevant features of the scene, and drawing conclusions from them. The ability to do this is clearly related to maturation and intelligence, and partly to knowledge, which, as we have seen, is culturally determined in a greater or lesser degree.

A child of the age of two or three years can identify and name correctly pictures of single objects; he can also recognise familiar objects in a more complicated picture. With increasing age he can enumerate in increasing detail the things he sees. At the age of seven he will normally be able to describe what is happening in a picture, but he would be incapable at that age of 'understanding' the meaning of a picture in which some complicated relationships of time, or cause and effect are represented. Such reading of a picture does not come until eleven or twelve. These facts are used by educational psychologists as one means of measuring a child's development.

'. . . Hello . . . Hello . . . '

For example, a child of eleven of average intelligence is just able to 'understand' the joke in this illustration, which depends upon recognising, firstly, the causal relation between an accident and the need to telephone, secondly, between the fact that the telephone wires are cut and the frustration depicted on the face of the woman, and finally, all of these with the impatient language of the caption.

This is what is meant by 'reading' a picture, the study of which has been done by workers at the Centre Audio Visuel de l'ENS de Saint-Cloud.[1] It can be taught, and learnt by a child, as they have shown in their experiments, where there was a marked improvement in 'reading' ability as the experiment proceeded.

It is important, however, to recognise, as Professor Vernon points out in this connection, that 'the teacher cannot assume that schoolchildren will readily understand what she teaches them simply because she shows them pictures.'[2]

Understanding, however, is not only a question of intelligence and maturity, but of *knowledge*. Unless, for example, we knew that telephone messages were carried along wires, we could not make the necessary connections between the relevant features of the last illustration to understand the joke. This type of knowledge is nowadays less and less culture-bound; but if we refer back to the illustration in Section 1, a knowledge that turkeys were eaten at Christmas in England would be a necessary bit of knowledge in order to 'see' the joke. An example of culturally determined knowledge. This fact links up with the point already made that *recognition* of relevant features may also be culturally determined. But the recognition of the bird as a turkey in this example is, in itself, not enough for understanding; the connection between the turkey and the 25th December must also be made, and this is what is involved in 'reading' or 'understanding' that particular picture.

In teaching, a picture, remember, serves as part of the situational context of the language taught. But we must equally 'read' and 'understand' a live situational context. When someone enters a room and looks around at what is happening, he may say,

[1] Guenot, Sturge-Moore and Tardy: 'Etudes sur la Lisibilité des Vues Fixes' in *Etudes de Linguistique Appliquée*, Didier, Paris, 1962.

[2] M. D. Vernon: op. cit.

eventually: 'Somebody tell me what is going on here?' Such a request shows that he has not 'read' the situation. He has perhaps not *seen* the relevant features; he has perhaps not *recognised* the features; he has certainly not *understood* their relationships or he would never have asked the question.

In our live situational teaching or in our use of visual materials and techniques, our pupils must never be put in the position of needing to ask: 'What is going on here?'

4

The Use of Visual Materials

Section I Situational Teaching

By Situational Teaching we mean the use of the classroom, and the people and things in it, as the situational context of the language we teach.

At this point it might be as well to remind ourselves of the relationship between the language skills and the notions of meaning we have developed. When we practise the organisational skills, we are teaching the formal structure of the language, the patterns of sound, grammar and vocabulary which are acceptable to the native speaker. We saw that the pronunciation practice, the grammar drills of substitution, conversion and completion and the various vocabulary exercises of the same sort are all practice in these organisational skills. But we also saw that the relationships we discover between the formal items in the language patterns were what we called the formal meaning of the language. Teaching the organisational skills is teaching formal meaning.

When we make use of the classroom and the people and things in it—that is, when we teach situationally, we are teaching the situational meaning of the language, and developing the semantic skill. The difficulty is that in ordinary classroom teaching we cannot easily practise these skills separately and in isolation from each other. Every time a pupil opens his mouth and utters an *original* sentence, he is practising all his linguistic skills, motor-perceptive, organisational and semantic. Note that we have said an *original* sentence; this qualification is necessary because there is no doubt that it is possible to utter lots of sentences without practising the semantic skill. This happens when we ask a pupil to read something beyond his capacity to understand. Indeed, we often do this ourselves in our mother-tongue. It is quite possible to read silently or even aloud a whole paragraph or a page without having the faintest idea of what it is all about. Our semantic skill was simply not being made use of. Much practice in the language laboratory is of this sort, for example, and in the purely phonetic pronunciation practice we have succeeded, many would think unwisely, in eliminating the semantic element, in creating a purely parrot-learning situation.

However, as we have said, in our ordinary everyday classroom teaching we tend to practise all the skills simultaneously. It may well be, of course, that the teacher has in mind the teaching of a particular bit of language, such as a new grammatical pattern. The practice he devises to teach this will, however, contain the elements of both the semantic and organisational skills, and he will move back and forth between situational type teaching, making use of the classroom, its equipment and the people in it, to the textbook and drill materials which are not situational and emphasise the formal part of the learning task. The example which follows is of such a 'combined' operation, making use of both situational and formal teaching. The piece of language the teacher has in mind to teach is the pattern: *to have something done by someone.* But since language in context cannot be confined to one grammatical structure, one item of pronunciation or vocabulary, the best situational teaching develops round what has been called a 'centre d'intérêt'; in the case of the following example, the barber's shop.

This example has not been devised with a particular syllabus in mind and consequently the language taught does not necessarily conform to any particular grading. Nor is it suggested that the procedures outlined should form the sole teaching activity over a period of consecutive lessons. It is rather intended to demonstrate how many of the familiar classroom activities, dramatisation, grammar drill, learning by heart, discussion and activity methods, can all be brought to bear on the presentation and practice of a fairly narrow range of vocabulary and one grammatical structure.

STAGE I
Visual materials
A pupil with long hair
A pupil with short hair
A pair of scissors

A pair of hair clippers
A barber's gown
A comb
A mirror

Procedure
Bring the pupils out in front of the class and talk with them about their hair and hair-cutting in general.

Language used
Look! John has long hair. His hair is long. Tom has short hair. His hair is short. John needs to have his hair cut. It's a long time since John had his hair cut. Tom has had his hair cut recently. John, when did you have your hair cut last?

Procedure
Teach the names of the barber's instruments by the usual ostensive methods

Language used
This is a pair of scissors, clippers etc.
This is a comb, a mirror.
What can I do with a pair of scissors?
I can cut hair, paper, cloth, etc.
Can I cut paper, cloth, hair with a pair of clippers?
We use a comb for combing the hair.
A barber uses a comb when he cuts our hair.
This is a barber's gown.
When does a barber use a gown?
When he's cutting our hair.
When do we wear a barber's gown?
When we are having our hair cut.

STAGE II
Visual materials
Barber's equipment
Picture of barber's shop (interior) No. 1.

Procedure
Re-teach mirror, comb, scissors, etc. Teach barber, barber's chair

and any other words needed. Teacher talks with pupils about the barber's shop.

THE BARBER'S SHOP

I

Language used

How many barbers are there in the shop?
What are they doing?
They are cutting the customers' hair.
What are they using?
What are the customers in the chairs doing?
They are having their hair cut.
Do you like having your hair cut?
Is it nice to have your hair cut?

Activity

Pupils will make their own visual aids out of cardboard; a mirror, comb and pair of scissors. Teacher talks to them individually while they are doing this.

Dialogue

Teacher goes over dialogue in class to make sure it is understood.

62

Dialogue

Mother: Oh, John! Your hair is too long. How long is it since you had it cut?

John: It must be about three weeks.

Mother: Well, I think its really time you had it cut again.

John: All right, mother. I'll have it cut straight away. Can I have some money, please?

Mother: How much does it cost?

John: Half-a-crown.

Mother: Here you are, dear. Don't be long.

Homework

Pupils learn dialogues by heart.

STAGE III

Visual materials

Home-made barber's equipment.

Pictures Nos. 2 and 3.

HE IS GOING TO HAVE HIS HAIR CUT

2

Procedures

Let several pairs of children act out the dialogue they have learned by heart. Teacher talks with pupils about the outside of the barber's shop.

Language to be used

How can you tell that this is a barber's shop?

It has a pole outside.
What is the pole like?
It has red and white spirals on it.
What do people do in barbers' shops?
They have (get) their hair cut.
What do people do in tailors' shops?
What do people do in carpenters' shops?

Activity

Pupils mime in pairs the cutting of a customer's hair, using their home-made equipment. Teacher moves around the class asking them questions about what they are doing.

Dialogue

Go over dialogue 2.

Dialogue 2

Barber: Good morning, sir. What can I do for you?
John: I want to have my hair cut.
Barber: Would you take a seat please. I have another customer.
John: Certainly.
Barber: Here's the newspaper to read while you're waiting to have your hair cut.
John: Oh, thank you.

Homework

Learn dialogue 2 by heart.

HE IS WAITING TO HAVE HIS HAIR CUT

3

STAGE IV
Visual materials
Pictures 4 and 5.

Procedures
Teacher talks with pupils about the inside of a barber's shop. Act dialogue 2.

4

HE IS HAVING HIS HAIR CUT

IT COST 2/6 TO HAVE HIS HAIR CUT

5

Language used
What is John waiting for?
He is waiting to have his hair cut.
Why is he waiting?

Because another customer is having his hair cut.

Do barbers make clothes?

Where do you go when you want to have a suit made?

Where do you go when you want to have a table made?

How much does it cost to have your hair cut?

Which costs more: to have your hair cut or to have your shoes mended?

How long does it take to have your hair cut?

Dialogue
Go over dialogue 3.

Dialogue 3
Barber: Next please, it's your turn now, sir.

John:　Thank you.

Barber: Now sir, how would you like it?

John:　Short back and sides please.

Barber: Certainly sir. Shall I take a little off the top?

John:　No thank you. Not this time.

Barber: Very well sir.

Homework
Learn dialogue 3 by heart.

STAGE V

Visual materials
Pictures 6, 7, 8 and 9.

Language used
The object of these materials is to give an opportunity to generalise the use of the grammatical pattern. The pictures are not for teaching vocabulary, and are used here solely in order that the formal learning shall also be meaningful.

Procedures
Act dialogue 3 as in previous stages.

Drills
Do the following practice drills in the grammar pattern. This is now purely formal learning.

6   7

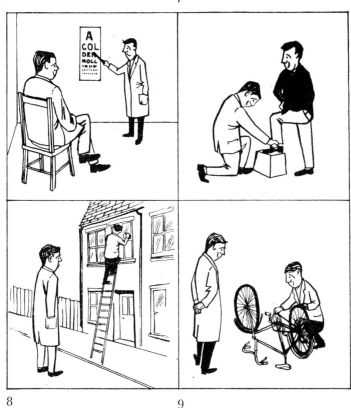

8   9

Conversion exercises

Change these sentences as in the examples:

    The barber is cutting John's hair

    He is having his hair cut (by the barber).

1. The painter is painting John's house.
2. The doctor is testing his eyes.
3. The mechanic is repairing William's bicycle.
4. The cobbler has mended all our shoes.
5. The shoe-shine boy is going to clean his shoes.
6. I want the tailor to make me a suit.
7. The gardener is going to cut our grass.

Completion exercises

Add a suitable word in the space so that the sentence makes good sense.

She is going to have her hair . . .
She is going to have her hair trimmed (washed, set).

1. He is going to have his windows . . .
2. He wants to have his puncture . . .
3. It costs £20 to have a new suit . . .
4. He had all his . . . corrected by the teacher.
5. It would be nice to have our house . . .
6. Mother wants to have the table . . .
7. I am waiting to have my . . . mended.
8. He's going to have his new house . . . by an architect.

Homework

Completion and conversion exercises to be written.

Section II Sound Film

As yet, little use has been made of sound film in the language classroom. Compared with the other materials we have been talking about there is very little language teaching material on film made specially for the purpose. The reasons for this are many.

The making of film is an expensive process. This means that the film when finished is expensive for schools to buy. Many will hesitate to do so unless they can see a clear advantage in the use of film for language teaching over other visual materials for the same ends. Similarly, film producers are likely to be reluctant to invest money in an expensive enterprise unless they can see a ready market for their productions.

Not only are films themselves expensive, but the means of showing them, the projectors, are also. Consequently many schools still lack a projector.

Even if a projector is available many teachers fight shy of operating it in the classroom because of their unfamiliarity with the techniques of doing so. They also begrudge the time necessary for preparing the classroom, blacking it out, threading and adjusting the projector, and setting up the screen. All these things are necessary unless the classroom is one which is especially equipped for the showing of film.

Furthermore, many teachers consider that the disruption of normal routine which the showing of films can mean is too high a price to pay for the learning that results. Some of these objections will no longer be valid when the 8 mm. cassette-loading sound film with magnetic sound track becomes readily available for educational use. With this equipment the teacher does not need to be a trained projectionist, no screen is needed and no blacking out is necessary. All that is required is that the teacher push a cassette into the rear-projection projector and turn on a switch. From the pupil's point of view the effect is very much like that of viewing television.[1]

One of the main objections hitherto to the use of 16 mm. sound film for language teaching has been the quality of the sound. The optical sound track rarely produces sound of the quality which is necessary for following a film in a foreign language, although it may be acceptable for the teaching of other subjects in the mother tongue. Here we may remember that in teaching a subject like science, language helps to explain what is seen, whereas in language teaching what is seen has to explain what is heard. Unless, therefore, the language is clearly heard the chances of understanding taking place are small. Here again, the introduction of magnetic sound track, such as we are familiar with in our sound tape recorders, is beginning to make this objection obsolete.

Perhaps as a result of these technical advances we shall see an increased use of sound film. But this is not yet at all certain since the most serious drawbacks to the use of film are pedagogical and linguistic.

The use of mechanical aids in the classroom is justified only if they can do something which the teacher unaided cannot do, or can do less effectively. The film can do one such thing; it can bring realistic contextualisation of language in situations which cannot otherwise be readily reproduced in the classroom. In other

[1] Forsdale and Dykstra: 'An Experimental Method of Teaching Foreign Languages by Means of 8-mm. sound film in cassette loading projectors,' *Language Learning* (Ann Arbor), 13, I, 1963, 5–10. The films made for this experiment are called: *English Face to Face*.

words, it can more completely demonstrate the meaning of a large amount of spoken language than any other means. But this very realism carries with it, from the teacher's point of view, a serious problem. Because the situation is realistic the language in it must also be realistic.

Language outside the classroom is not controlled or restricted in the same way as the language presented in a teaching course must be. For this reason it is scarcely possible to write a realistic film script which does not constantly go outside the linguistic range of all but fairly advanced students. Any attempt on the part of the script writer to restrict his language to a point in a particular syllabus leads to a greater or lesser degree of exoticism in the situations presented. The script writer has to think up some fairly unusual scene to accommodate the rather abnormal language. This defeats the prime purpose of the film, since an exotic situation is not one which most learners can use to understand the language; and this, after all, is the purpose of contextualisation. How then to make use of such film material in which the dialogue constantly goes beyond the learner's knowledge?

Unless film can offer considerable learning opportunities, the disruption its showing entails is not worth while. This disruption means that it is also not worth while to show any film which lasts only a minute or so. A minimum length of, say, ten to fifteen minutes might start paying off. Here we have another dilemma for the film maker and teacher. The sheer amount of language that must occur in ten minutes is likely to be overwhelming for the learner. There are two possible remedies for this situation. First, that most of the film shall be silent and shall be taken up with action of a non-linguistic sort; in such a case one would be paying for a lot of material which would be only marginally concerned with language teaching and consequently the cost of such a film would not be justified. The second solution is so to script the film that it has a high degree of repetition of the same or similar language material. Except in rather unusual circumstances this does not happen in real life in consecutive action, although in discontinuous scenes it could be made to. Here the skill of the script writer will help. He may be able to find a series of scenes in which there is much repetition of language, but which are sufficiently different from each other situationally not to offend the learner's sense of realism or to bore him by their similarity.

Film is something which is normally watched in silence. It only provides practice in comprehension, thus it exercises only one aspect of the semantic skill. Many teachers would regard this as an expensive way of doing the job. It would seem justified only inasmuch as the linguistic material presented belonged in situational contexts which could otherwise not be convincingly simulated in the classroom.

Even if all the objections to film so far presented could be overcome, the expense of using film to do fifteen minutes comprehension practice would still not be justified. Film must therefore do more; it must serve as the starting point of a series of learning activities. A language-teaching film must present enough material of the right sort and in the right way to warrant it being shown to the same class on several occasions. This implies that the learners can bear to see it more than once, simply *as a film*. No pupil is going to learn anything from a film he is bored by. Instead of it being a valuable motivating factor, it will be exactly the opposite. But to make a fifteen-minute film which can stand watching several times requires considerable inventiveness and ingenuity on the part of the script writer and producer.

The result of all these factors is that the little film material that has been made for language teaching is designed for revision and comprehension practice at intermediate and advanced levels of language learning, or that it has been designed as merely one element in a planned audio-visual course.[1]

As an example of a film intended to stand on its own we may take *What's the Time?* This film was designed for second or third year learners of English in European secondary schools. It is a film for the revision of the language of telling and asking the time.

Here are the *Notes for the Teacher* which accompany the film whose method of use they describe.[2]

[1] Such a 'package-deal' course, consisting of textbooks, film-strips, tapes, records and films is: 'El Español por el Mundo', Encyclopaedia Britannica Films Inc., Illinois, 1964.

[2] *What's the Time?*, a film made by Basic Films Ltd. (producer: John Krish) for the British Council. This film won the Gold Plaque at the Educational Film and Television Festival in Rome, 1962.

What's the Time?

1 The aim of this film is to show the principal ways of asking and telling the time as they occur in the contexts of real life; that is, to show where and when each form is properly used, the social and situational conditions in which it is appropriate.

2 In the ordinary language course the student learns the forms he may use and how to formulate them grammatically and in pronunciation, but he less often learns *when* these forms should be used. It is difficult in the classroom to demonstrate this without elaborate play-acting. Film comes in because it can show language as it is actually used in life.

3 This film is not intended for the presentation of linguistic forms which the student does not yet know. It aims to teach the student when he may use the forms which he has already learnt.

4 It would be possible to describe in words to the student the characteristics of the situations in which particular forms occurred. This would be time-consuming and, in any case, rather imprecise; it is much better to show live situations and let the student draw his own conclusions from them. The examples in the film reinforced by the guidance of the teacher will be more effective than laborious explanations.

5 Teachers may think that there is a lot of inessential material, visual and spoken, in the film. The visual material is necessary to establish the situations in which the language occurs: the language material is only part of the situation. It has been kept to a minimum, but in order to simulate *real* living situations some language is bound to be used which may be more or less unfamiliar to the learner. This is unavoidable because in real life language is not simplified as it is in the classroom; and to limit it to what is found in the textbooks at any particular stage would be to distort life, and to destroy the principal teaching of the film.

6 The material in the film can be divided into several categories of linguistic items varying in importance. Because we are

simulating real life, the items are distributed through the film. It is the teacher's job to point out, to practise and to consolidate the items in the relevant category *before* each showing of the film.

7 The way to use this film, then, is to show it a number of times. Before each showing the particular category of linguistic items to which the students' attention is to be drawn should be studied. All other material can be overlooked; its turn will come. There should be little difficulty in adopting this procedure, since the familiar situations presented here should make the language used perfectly comprehensible in a general sense. Detailed study of the whole script at one time should not be necessary and indeed is, from a teaching point of view, undesirable. This is a film to study, and the study should proceed systematically over a number of showings. Each showing should be used to reveal a new series of linguistic items. The design of the film is based upon the assumption that it would be shown several times, and the content was made sufficiently interesting and varied to stand frequent viewing without the students being bored.

The film itself is a story about a mother and her son of twelve years who have a train to catch. The mother is a nervous person who is afraid that they will miss the train. From the moment the story begins in their house to the time they arrive by taxi at the station she is asking her son the time. She is, however, not satisfied that his watch is right and takes every opportunity of asking the time of others: the taxi-driver, the drivers of other cars and the booking clerk. Her son is a much calmer person and finds his mother's anxiety rather insufferable. Even when she finds that they have arrived half an hour too early at the station she is still uneasy. This perhaps not entirely probable situation gives the opportunity for introducing naturally a large number of the commoner ways of asking and telling the time, and for talking about time.

It is suggested to teachers in the accompanying notes that the film should be shown at least five times. This is the linguistic material to be practised and studied at each showing. All quotations are from the dialogue of the film:

FIRST SHOWING: WAYS OF ASKING THE TIME

1 'What time is it?'
'What time is your train?'
This is the neutral form. It is suitable for all situations.

2 'What's the time?'
This is also a neutral form, perhaps a little more informal.

3 'Have you the (right) time (on you)?'
The person who asks this is not sure that the person asked has a watch.
'Have you the time?' is used, but is more often found with 'right' or such as phrase as 'on you' or 'by any chance'.

4 'What time do you make it?'
More often asked by someone who has a watch himself but cannot rely on its accuracy or wishes to check it.

5 'Got the time?'
This is rather a familiar form; even more familiar than 'Have you got the time?'

6 'Any idea of the time?'
This, too, is very familiar.

7 'Can you tell me what the time is?'
This is a formal way of asking the time. Used to strangers and older people. It may be compared with 'Would you tell me what time it is?' or 'Can you tell me the time?'

8 'What time did you say it was?'
Is an indirect repetition of 'What time is it?'
'What time did you say the train was?'
Is an indirect repetition of 'What time is the train?'

SECOND SHOWING: WAYS OF TELLING THE TIME
There are two ways of telling the time; this showing deals with the first way. Both ways may be introduced by such forms as:

1 'It's . . .'
'You told me it was (indirect form)'

2 'My watch/clock says . . .'

3 'I make it . . .'

The first states the time confidently. Both 2 and 3 suggest some qualification: that the speaker only knows what his watch tells him. Any of these opening forms may be used with any of the question forms 1–8. For example:

'What time is it?' 'My watch says . . .'

'What time do you make it?' 'It's . . .'

'Have you the right time?' 'I make it . . .'

4 Using 'past' and 'to'.
  a with *half* and *quarter* and *o'clock*
quarter past nine	quarter to ten
half past nine	quarter to twelve
ten o'clock	

  b with multiples of five minutes
ten to ten	ten minutes past twelve
ten past twelve	

  c with units of individual minutes. The word 'minute(s)' must be used in these cases:
two minutes past	four minutes to ten
one minute to ten	nine minutes to one

  d without the 'hour'
  When the speaker believes the listener knows the nearest whole hour, he need not mention it:
nearly five past	two minutes past
nearly half past	

The form studied in this showing may be considered as the usual form of stating the time. It is the neutral form. Note the rather old-fashioned formal 'four minutes past the hour'.

THIRD SHOWING: WAYS OF TELLING THE TIME
  'Timetable' method of telling the time.
  A speaker tends to use this method when he has an event

75

which has a fixed starting time in mind, such as the departure of a train, the time of an appointment or the start of a lesson.

ten fifteen, ten thirty, ten forty-five
eleven thirty-two
twelve ten, twelve twenty
eleven thirty
eleven forty-five

FOURTH SHOWING: CLOCKS AND WATCHES: 'FAST', 'SLOW' AND 'RIGHT'

Clocks and watches are not always right and need to be put right. There is a group of expressions which are used in these circumstances. Either a watch is 'going' or 'has stopped'. If it 'is going' it may be going 'fast' or 'slow'.
At any moment it may be 'fast', 'slow' or 'right'.

a 'My watch has stopped.'
'It's stopped again.'

'My watch has stopped'

b 'My watch may be fast.'
  'The kitchen clock is slow.'
  'It's probably fast.'
  'Well, fast or slow, it's not right.'
  'Station clocks are always right.'
  'Is it right?'
  'My watch never *loses* a minute or *gains* a minute.'

c 'I didn't *wind* it.'
  'Don't *overwind* it.'
  'I'm sure you *overwound* it.'
  'I *set the hands*.'
  'I only *set* the *hands*.'
  '*Put* it *right* for me.'

d 'Is that the right time?'
  'Find out what the right time is.'
  'To ask whether it's the *correct* time or not.'

Note: both a watch and the 'time' may be right, but usually 'correct' is only used with 'time'. 'Is that the right time?' questions whether the watch is telling the $\begin{cases} \text{right} \\ \text{correct} \end{cases}$ time.

We can then say: 'Is your watch right?'

FIFTH SHOWING: 'LATE', 'HAVING TIME', 'HURRYING'.

If we are not late for an appointment we are either 'early' or 'in time'.

a 'We're going to be terribly late.'
  'We're going to be late.'
  'The train leaves half an hour later.'
  'So you're *in* plenty of *time*.' (not late)

b 'There won't be time.'
  'There's plenty of time.'
  'If there's time.'
  'Plenty of time now.'

have time (to), *have got time (to . . .)*
c 'We may have time to stop. . . .'

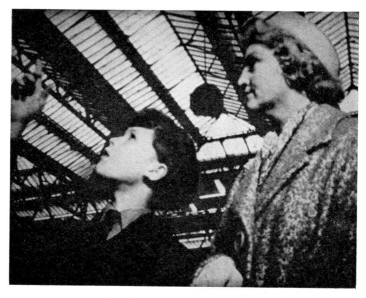

'Station clocks are always right'

'We'll have an hour to wait.'
'We've only got twenty minutes to. . . .'
'We've got ten minutes.'
'Do you think we've got time.'

hurry

d 'We won't have to hurry.'
'Hurry now!'
'You'll have to hurry.'

e 'It'll take hours (to . . .).'

'Hours' means a long time and is familiar in style. The exact time something takes to perform can be stated. It takes half an hour/several days/etc. (to . . .).

Section III Audio-visual Courses

Teaching languages by what is often nowadays called simply *the* audio-visual method has expanded rapidly in recent years. This
78

method has proved itself to be particularly effective when teaching adults the spoken skills in intensive courses. The name 'audio-visual' is entirely appropriate—as it would be to all methods described in this chapter—since it relies on a combined use of projected still pictures and recorded speech.

As we saw in the last chapter, these materials are nowadays more usually designed to be largely self-contained, in the sense that the role of the classroom teacher is secondary. The best results are often obtained when at least some part of the learning is done in the language laboratory, where the students have play-back facilities so that they can monitor their own productive practice. This further reduces the participation of the teacher in the learning process.

There is no reason, of course, why projected still pictures accompanied by recorded speech should not be used as support material to other classroom teaching activities, and indeed this was done before the technique which is to be described was developed. In this technique the language material is presented as recorded speech. This may take the form of a commentary on projected pictures, or it may be a dialogue for which the pictures are a contextualisation. Or it may consist of a mixture of both of these. In this respect the choices are the same as in the making of a cine film. The vital difference being that the presentation can proceed at a far slower speed. It can even permit repetition or return to earlier stages. Consequently the resulting material will fulfil different teaching functions.

The commentary style speech would seem to be a less satisfactory procedure since, apart from an authoritative pronunciation, which all recorded speech material can have, there does not seem to be anything that this technique can do which the teacher himself cannot do as well or even better in his own classroom. This is certainly one of the reasons why the dialogue speech technique seems to be establishing itself.

These dialogues normally consist of a series of short utterances of one or two sentences, rarely more, each spoken by one of the participants. These, also, rarely number more than three, since a larger number would lead to a greater difficulty in identifying who is speaking, and hence to slower comprehension. Each utterance is illustrated by a projected drawing, not a photograph, for reasons which will be clear from the argument in the previous chapter. The picture, by careful design and taken in conjunction with previous pictures in the sequence is intended fully to contextualise the language heard with it.

Teaching procedures in the 'audio-visual method' normally follow a course like this:

First phase, in which the pupils practise the receptive skills. The lesson sequence is presented several times in succession until the language is fully understood. The teacher's job here is to satisfy himself by one means or another that all the learners have indeed understood all the language presented. To proceed without this assurance is to invite parrot-learning.

Second phase. This is the phase which may be carried out with good effect in the language laboratory in the case of the adult student. Each utterance in the dialogue is presented several times. The students imitate it after each repetition, all the time looking at the picture so that the utterance *remains* meaningful, and the activity does not degenerate into parrot-learning. The students' practice can be individually recorded and later self-monitored, or the teacher can monitor each student's practice in turn, this being normal language laboratory technique.

Third phase. Here the pictures are presented again, but without the recorded sound. Now the pupils must speak the dialogue from memory, matching their utterances to the pictures as they appear. In a classroom situation this phase develops naturally into free conversation practice if there is a trained teacher to conduct it.

The language material presented by this technique must, of course, be very carefully selected and graded, and each dialogue, apart from presenting the language belonging to a 'centre d'intérêt', can also be selected and organised so that a particular grammatical or phonological point is taught and practised. The difficulties of designing such dialogues are akin to those outlined in the previous section concerned with writing scripts for films; but they are less acute since departures from realism are likely to be better tolerated when contextualisation itself is done by drawings rather than cine-photography. The problems of designing an audio-visual course are most acute in the matter of making

a

Enlevez votre manteau

e

Oui, il est dans son bureau

b

Accrochez-le ici

f

Michel, c'est Jacques

c

Merci

g

Ah, bonjour, Jacques

d

Est-ce-que Michel est là?

h

Je viens tout de suite

illustrations which can be rapidly 'read' without misunderstanding. The difficulties of doing this have been discussed in the previous chapter.

The specimen material on page 81 is taken from an audio-visual course prepared by C.R.E.D.I.F.[1] and is part of the fifth lesson in a series of thirty-two lessons for teaching spoken French to foreign adult learners. It represents only part of the first phase of a lesson—the presentation of the language in the form of a 'sketch' —and is to be followed by two further dialogues which concentrate attention and practice on points of grammar and pronunciation.

Section IV Television

As we saw in the preceding chapter, the classroom teacher has virtually no control over television teaching except whether to turn on the receiver or not. In its simplest form TV is no more than an electronic means of transferring image and sound from one place to another, and, if recording is used, from one time to another. Since this is so, what the television teacher does in front of the camera may be no more than what the classroom teacher does in front of his class. This is the most primitive use that can be made of television and has earned the name of *televised instruction*, since it makes no attempt to use those special facilities that TV can offer and which do not exist in the classroom. If this was the only use made of television in language teaching, there would be no justification for including a section on it in this book, since any visual techniques the TV teacher might use—situational teaching, blackboard, or even film—would already have been discussed.

What we are here concerned with is the visual techniques which TV can offer which are not available to the classroom teacher. A TV language lesson employing these techniques might take the form of a dramatic episode in the foreign language, in which case

[1] Centre de Recherches et d'Etudes pour la Diffusion du Français, Ecole Normale Supérieure de Saint-Cloud. The name of the course is 'Voix et Images de France'. The agent in Britain is G. Harrap, London.

nothing could be less like the traditional classroom language lesson. In such a programme the learner might feel that he was witnessing a 'slice of life' from another country, language, customs, culture and all. Indeed this might be exactly what he had seen. Language teaching programmes of both these extreme kinds, and of every intermediate stage between them have been produced, and deserve the name *instructional television.*[1]

The role that television can play in language teaching is unique. It may set out to teach individual learners in their own homes or to teach classes in schools; it may set out to help the qualified language teacher in his classroom to present language which he cannot, for technical reasons, present unaided. In this function it resembles the use of film. Or it may set out to teach pupils in a school where there is no qualified teacher at all.

TV is totally independent of classroom teacher and learner. Indeed the TV producer and teacher do not know from moment to moment whether they even have an audience. This fact serves to emphasise the most severe limitation that TV suffers from in comparison with conventional teaching. As we have seen, language involves at least two participants, speaker and hearer. In situational teaching these are selected from amongst the teacher and his pupils in the classroom. But TV is a one-way type of communication; the teacher can talk to the pupil, but the pupil cannot talk to the teacher. Certainly conversation can be shown on TV, but then the learner is in the position not of a participant but of an eavesdropper.

Although TV language teaching appears to take a large variety of forms, we can, nevertheless, discern three main sorts of teaching jobs it may do.

First of all it may undertake to teach those who have no other teacher. These learners may be at home or in school, such teaching function has been called 'whole teaching'.

Then there is the programme which is directed to school learners whose language teacher is either untrained or has only rudimentary training. Such teachers may have some ability in

---

[1] For a fuller discussion of the distinction between televised instruction and instructional television, see S. P. Corder: *English Language Teaching and Television*, pp. 1-2, Longmans, 1961.

the language but no knowledge of teaching method or descriptive knowledge of the language being taught. With guidance from the TV centre in the form of notes and suggested procedures, and with the support of recorded language material and books they are able to do useful but limited follow-up practice with the learner in his classroom. This sort of programme is called 'part teaching' although the main burden for the presentation of the language falls upon the TV teacher.[1]

The third sort of programme is that which merely supplements already adequate teaching. It may have motivational reasons behind it, or it may have general cultural intention; in which case it is best regarded as 'enrichment' rather than strictly language teaching. Such programmes take the form of dramatic episodes in the foreign language or documentary programmes about life and culture in the country whose language is being studied. In neither case is there necessarily anyone who appears on the screen who can be identified as the teacher.

The type of programme that may be adopted to meet any particular teaching situation will be dependent to a large extent upon the amount of money that is available to the TV teacher and producer. TV production is expensive. The capital and running costs of a TV station or studio are high before ever a programme is devised, and money for educational programmes always seems to be scarce. Yet what TV can especially offer to the language teacher, that is, naturalistic contextualisation of language, involves the most expensive production procedures—long rehearsal time, trained actors, larger studio staff and more expensive equipment and lighting, costly scenery and perhaps even costumes and make-up. Thus, though it has no doubt been the ambition of all those who have taught languages by TV to avail themselves of TV's contextualising capacity, cost has in most cases frustrated these desires to a greater or lesser extent. In the event, then, most TV language teaching has fallen back upon the teacher, visual materials of a more or less conventional sort, and, as an occasional luxury, some modest attempt at situational

[1] For a study of such a teaching programme see: Garry and Mauriello: *Summary of Research on 'Parlons Français'*, Years I, II and III, Modern Language Project, Massachusetts Council for Public Schools, Boston, 1960-62.

contextualisation, using what local resources in amateur dramatics might be available.

It is from such a language teaching programme that the following example is chosen.[1]

Do you Mind?

Fade in title
DO YOU MIND?
Mix to: Teacher

Teacher

Hallo, schools. Today we're going to talk about the word MIND. This word has a lot of different meanings, as you probably know. We talk of a MAN'S MIND, or HAVE YOU ANYTHING IN MIND?, or I HAVE A MIND TO DO SOMETHING. Or, for example, we say SHE IS MINDING THE BABY WHILE HER MOTHER IS OUT, or we talk about a man MINDING A MACHINE.

But today we are not going to deal with these words or meanings; today we are going to show you how we use the word TO MIND when it means something like to OBJECT TO or TO HAVE AN OBJECTION TO.

But let's see what our friends Dele and Akin are doing.

Cut to: Two schoolboys doing their homework just before setting off for school

Teacher (Out of vision)

Dele and Akin are just finishing their homework. They have to leave for school in five minutes, so they're in a hurry. You remember how forgetful Dele

[1] This programme was broadcast experimentally over the Schools Television programme in Ibadan, Nigeria, on 10th November, 1960. Producer, George Arms.

is. Well, he left all his books and other things at school yesterday. I don't know what his teacher will say!

Dele

Oh, dear! I've left my pen at school. What shall I do? I shall never finish my homework in time. Akin, would you mind lending me yours? I promise I won't spoil it.

Akin

Oh, all right. Here you are. I don't mind so long as you don't break it. Do hurry up with it, though. I haven't finished my own homework yet and we only have ten minutes left.

Cut to: Teacher

Teacher

Now, one of the interesting things about this word is that it is used most often in only one or two fixed expressions. These expressions are negative sentences or questions. You will rarely hear it used in affirmative sentences. Let's pick out the example we just heard. . . .

Cut to: Caption

DO YOU	
WOULD YOU	MIND
I DON'T	

Cut to: Teacher

Teacher

Let's see how Dele and Akin are getting on with their homework, shall we?

Cut to: Boys

Dele

Oh! Now I've made a mistake. Akin, do you mind letting me use your rubber? I left mine at school, I think.

Akin

Here you are. Take it. Anything else you want?

86

Cut to : Teacher

Teacher

Another thing we can learn about TO MIND is that it is often followed by an -ING form of the verb: words like DOING, MAKING or, as we have just heard, LENDING or LETTING.

Cut to : Captions

Cut to : Boys
DELE IS HUMMING A TUNE

Akin

Oh, Dele, for Heaven's sake! Do you mind not making that awful noise? I'm trying to read.

Dele

What? . . . Oh, sorry, Akin. I was only singing. I can think better when I sing. Do you really mind?

Akin

Yes, I do.

Cut to : Caption

┌─────────────────────┐
│ DO YOU MIND NOT │
│ MAKING THAT AWFUL   │
│ NOISE?   │
└─────────────────────┘

Cut to : Teacher

Teacher

All the examples we have heard so far have been showing the word MIND in sentences requesting someone to do something, or not to do something, politely. Notice—POLITELY.

But we also use the word MIND when we ask someone their permission to do something ourselves.

G

Let's have another look at Dele and Akin and see what they're up to now, shall we?

Cut to: Boys

Dele

Oh, Akin, would you mind if I borrowed your ruler? I can't find mine anywhere. I think I must have left it at school, with my pen and my rubber and . . .

Akin

. . . yes, and your history book and your geography book and all your other school things! All right. I don't mind, but remember to give it me back before we go to school.

Cut to: Teacher

Teacher

I do think Akin is very patient, don't you? Do you remember what Dele said? WOULD YOU MIND IF I BORROWED YOUR RULER? Of course he could have said WOULD YOU MIND MY BORROWING YOUR RULER? It means the same thing. Look at these examples. . . .

Cut to: Caption

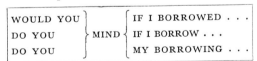

Teacher (out of vision)

Yes, you must be careful here. If you use WOULD YOU MIND, you have to use the past tense BORROWED. But if you use DO YOU MIND you must use the present tense BORROW.

Cut to: Boys
AS AKIN SPEAKS HE
TAKES BACK HIS PEN,
RULER AND RUBBER
AND GETS UP TO GO.

Akin
If you don't mind, I'll have my pen

'If you don't mind, I'll have my pen back'

back . . . and my ruler . . . and my
rubber. I'm going to school now. I don't
want to be late. I suppose you don't
mind being late.

DELE RISES ALSO, LEAV-
ING BEHIND A BOOK

Dele
Hey! Wait a moment! I'm just coming.
Don't go without me!
Akin
Come along then. Hurry up!

Cut to: Teacher
Teacher
In the example we have just seen, Akin
wasn't asking Dele to do anything for

89

him. He did it himself. He certainly wasn't asking Dele's permission to do anything. He just snatched up his pen, his rubber and his ruler, didn't he? You may be thinking he wasn't very polite. Perhaps you're right.

We often say IF YOU DON'T MIND before we do something. It's generally a way of warning someone that we are going to do it *whether he likes it or not*. It's the way that we say it that makes it polite or not. Listen to these examples:

Cut to: Caption

IF YOU DON'T MIND, I'LL JUST HAVE MY PEN BACK

Voice over

(Menacingly) If you don't mind. I'll just have my pen back.
(Politely) If you don't mind, I'll just have my pen back.

Cut to: Teacher

Teacher

Before we end the programme, let's just see if those boys have left for school yet, shall we?

Cut to: Table at which boys were
BOYS HAVE GONE, BUT THERE IS A BOOK LYING ON THE TABLE

Push in to close up of book
Cut to: Teacher

Teacher

Oh, dear. I might have guessed that Dele would leave his homework behind!

Goodbye schools.

Fade out to end titles

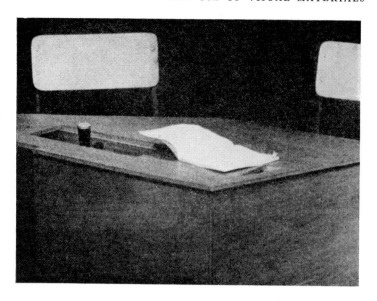

'I might have known Dele would forget his homework'

Conclusion

Visual methods in language teaching have come in very quickly; their introduction has been hastened by the development of the electronic and mechanical means for displaying visual materials. Forty years ago, apart from what the individual teacher may have done to make use of the visible features of the classroom situation for language teaching, visual techniques, if they deserved the name, were confined to rudimentary textbook illustrations or blackboard drawings. Now, new visual materials appear on the market almost monthly. It is perhaps appropriate, therefore, at this point to sit back a moment and review the state of affairs.

There is no reason to suppose that there will be any slackening now in the production of new material for what have become established media, film, filmstrip, wall picture and television. We have already noted that the production costs of these materials can be very high. This is so not because the raw materials themselves are expensive, but because the techniques of preparation, usually involving large technical staff and resources, are costly, and because, when such an investment is undertaken, it is important for the producer that the material remain relevant and up to date for as long as period as possible. This involves further costly investment in testing and validating the material. But we live in an era when education is receiving more attention on the part of peoples and governments than ever before. This interest is being followed, however slowly, by increased funds for educational purposes, teachers, buildings and instructional materials. It is reasonable to expect that expensive materials, machinery and techniques will, so long as they continue to prove their worth, become more and more widespread in use.

But we cannot expect that we have reached the end of the inventions in this field. One new development—the advent of the 8 mm. magnetic sound track cassette-loading film—has already been mentioned. Other technical developments are also under way; for example, the sound sensitive relay which causes the next frame in a film strip to be screened as soon as the learners have finished repeating the language of the previous frame. All new minor technical discoveries—and the ones mentioned are both in a technical sense only minor developments—may nevertheless have quite disproportionate effects upon learning and teaching methods, as Forsdale and Dykstra say in their article on the 8 mm. sound film.[1]

It is quite prudent, then, to visualise the day, before many months have passed, when it will be technically possible for a learner . . . to retire to a language laboratory, a corner of a classroom, the central school library or some likely spot, to use motion pictures that can be readily operated *under his own control* as a learning resource. (My italics.)

I have added the italics in this quotation in order to emphasise the fact that the tendency of most of the recent developments in audio and visual material and techniques has been to place more and more of the responsibility for conducting his own learning upon the learner. One has only to think of those two major inventions, the language laboratory and programmed instruction, to see this trend most clearly.

Another trend which we would be prudent to expect to continue is the trend towards a combining of various techniques, audio and visual. We must expect combined use of audio-visual course and television, of television and film, of language laboratory and television, of film strip and programmed instruction, of programmed instruction and television, and so on. Some of these have already been tried, some are being experimented with now, some have yet to be investigated. Over all there looms the enigmatic shadow of the computer. For most language teachers this is still a research tool for the linguist, but we cannot close our eyes to the fact that a computer will come into teaching, and with it more changes than we now care to contemplate.

Many teachers may be dismayed when they consider these things. For some the pace of innovation has already been too great; some even shrink from the use of some of the materials and techniques which have been described in this book. It is, however, the duty of any teacher who aspires to be competent in the mod-

[1] Forsdale and Dykstra: op. cit.

ern techniques of his profession to learn as a minimum the simple domestic skills of operating film and film-strip projectors, tape-recorders, gramophones, language laboratories, and television sets; for he will soon be expected to handle sophisticated teaching machines and computers. But the skill in simple manipulation is only a preliminary step; it is one which every teacher will have to learn to take eventually. Operating a projector efficiently, however, is not of itself teaching by audio-visual techniques. The second step is to come to terms with the inevitable changes that the advent of these machines will bring, both in teaching materials and teaching techniques and, above all and most difficult to accept, in the function of the teacher in the whole educational process. We cannot ever expect that the teacher shortages which are being experienced in the present day in most countries in the world will ever be overcome by simply increasing the supply of teachers. The supply of teachers will, of course, be increased, but demand for teachers is always likely to outstrip supply. The problems of man-power can be met only by the use of machinery to do some of the work at present done by teachers; some of this machinery already exists and much more yet remains to be invented. If there is any truth in this assessment, then teachers of the future must accept a changing role in the instructional process.

None of these observations in any way affects the thesis of this book; whatever new sections must be added from year to year to Chapter 4, the functions of visual materials and techniques in language teaching will not change; they will always be concerned with the teaching of meaning.

But increased efficiency in the teaching of meaning must not come from more efficient techniques and tools alone; it must come from a better understanding of the relationship between language and situational context discussed in Chapter 3. The linguistic theories which handle this aspect of language are still primitive. Much work remains to be done on discovering the systematic nature of this relationship. This is one of the great tasks of the applied linguist of the future. At present, language teaching courses are almost without exception linguistically based. In other words, what has been chosen for teaching is an inventory of linguistic items, in grammar, vocabulary and pronunciation.

95

This has been ordered largely according to linguistic criteria and then, and only then, have the means, visual or otherwise, been sought to make this mass of material meaningful.

One can perfectly well envisage theoretically a course which had as its starting point an inventory of situations in which the learner would have to learn to behave verbally. These situations would be analysed into catagories, some of which would be behavioural, and then, and only then, would the actual linguistic items be specified to make the situations meaningful. Such a procedure is foreseen by Professor Allen:

It is possible to imagine a linguistics in which the emphasis would be reversed—in which one noted primarily differences in situation, and supported these by differences in phonic events: two situations would then be different only if they involve differences in phonic events—a ram would be different from a lamb only because /r/ differed from /l/, and present would be different from past because, *inter alia*, the /z/ of *has* differed from /d/ of *had*.[1]

But we are far from a realisation of this ambition. Even intuitively we are only able to predict linguistic events with a better degree of success than chance in a very limited number of situations. Until the applied linguist has investigated in far greater detail and on a far wider scale what people actually say in what sort of situation, our predictive abilities will not rise much. And yet for visual methods of teaching this is the information for which above all, we are waiting. We can only hope that the applied linguist will make as important a contribution in the future as the electronic and mechanical engineers have done in the past.

[1] W. S. Allen: *On the Linguistic Study of Languages: An Inaugural Lecture*, C.U.P., 1957.